Endorsements

"A warmly written account of relationships with the dying. An inspirational and informational assessment important for anyone in Hospice care or anyone involved in personal care of the dying."

~ Suzanne Cuff, CNA

"Live with Purpose: Die with Dignity *is a book I simply could not put down. In each story the author shares a different experience of what it is like to be a hospice volunteer. The writing is descriptive and the words flow from the heart; I felt like I was sharing the experiences. I intend to use this book as a reference for our volunteer trainings.*

"I would recommend this book to anyone who wonders what it is like to walk beside a person who faces a terminal illness."

~ Criss East, Coordinator of Volunteers
Evergreen Hospice and Palliative Care
Kirkland, Washington

"As a fellow writer, I have been privileged to read Christina Lufkin's manuscript as the chapters unfold. I am now in my late 80's and am grateful to know through Christina's experiences that Hospice will be here for me when I need it."

~ Willma Gore Author,

Memoir, Iron Grip

"As a past Hospice occupational therapist volunteer, I was impressed with how succinct, and accurately Chris was able to convey her experiences with clients. It is daunting to go into a home where death is looming over a family, become part of that environment and bring some peace, comfort, understanding and joy into this difficult time. In this little book, you can witness the fear, compassion, and peace that comes from giving what you can from your heart and loving the persons involved in a non-judgmental way. I feel that this sharing will help others thinking of being part of hospice. It will encourage new volunteers to do what they can. None of us is an expert, but we all can love and learn to give as Chris did by just opening our hearts and doing our best . . . It is enough and it helps others immensely. Enjoy this helpful book."

~ Verna Sak,

Retired Registered Occupational Therapist

Live with Purpose:

Live with Purpose:

Die with Dignity

To Dr. Iversen & Team,

With Gratitude,

Christina M. Lufkin

Christina Lufkin

Sacred Life Publishers™
SacredLife.com
Printed in the United States of America

≈ ≈

Live with Purpose: Die with Dignity

Copyright © 2011

You may purchase a copy of *Live with Purpose: Die with Dignity* through your local bookstores, Amazon or other online bookstores, christinalufkin1@yahoo.com, or at SacredLife.com.

ISBN: 0-9822331-4-6
ISBN: 978-0-9822331-4-6
Library of Congress Control Number: 2011930455

The information, ideas, and suggestions in this book are not intended as a substitute for professional advice. Before following any suggestions contained in this book, consult your physician or mental health professional. Neither the author nor the publisher shall be liable or responsible for any loss or damage allegedly arising as a consequence of your use or application of any information or suggestions in this book.

Cover and text design: Miko Radcliffe at drawingacrowd.net
Photo of Christina Lufkin by: Marie Kokinos

Sacred Life Publishers™
SacredLife.com
Printed in the United States of America

Contents

Section 1 – Hospice: Discovery and Life's Purpose

Section 2 – My Patients' Stories

ᐃ   ᐁ

Section 3 – Final Thoughts

This book is dedicated

with much love to

Cleon A. Peterson,

June 28, 1917-December 25, 2004.

Your love of life and determination

to live life to the fullest,

while serving others, inspires me.

I miss you, although

I feel your presence with me!

இ   ஒ

Acknowledgements

This book would not be possible without the encouragement and support of my husband Dave, our daughter, Ivey, for your creative input, the Hospice patients and their families, co-volunteers, Hospice staff, my family and friends.

Thank you to Michael Ezell for your guidance, Chaplain Adam Bissell, at Hospice of the Pines, for your enthusiastic encouragement, Dan Sapienza for your assistance, and to Eng Tan for believing in me.

A special thanks to my publisher, Sharon Lund, Scared Life Publishers. My editor and author Willma Gore, *"Iron Grip, a Memoir,"* and author Robert Wood, *"Peaceful Passing"*.

I am extremely grateful to all of you.

Introduction

To live your purpose is to do what you love. We are all born with intuition, a gut feeling about where we are going and what we should do along the way. If each of us follows that inner voice it will lead us to what our life purpose is. You will know you are doing your life work if it feels right and good to you. If you have a passion and are excited about what you are doing, then you are living with purpose.

I have a close friend who, at the age of four, told his parents that he was going to be a pastor. He didn't say that he wanted to be a pastor; he announced that he would be one. He did become a pastor and has continued to be of service to others in many other ways as well as serving as a pastor. That is a great example of living with purpose that will lead to a dignified death. This pastor never allows others to steer him off course. I am sure that when he nears the end of his life here on earth he will make his own choices. He inspires me daily.

If you work in a job basically for the pay check you are not living with purpose. It is not likely to bring satisfaction for you.

Dying with dignity means to have no regrets at the end of your life. By defining to others or only to yourself what your purpose is, loving those in your life, and reconciling with anyone with whom you have disagreed, you will have a peaceful passing. All you have to do to live a life of purpose with no regrets is to decide to do so!

My life purpose is service to others. I found my calling with Hospice. My interest started when a friend told us about her experiences as a volunteer. She helped my Mother and me as my Dad was dying, in the summer of 1983. We were all very grateful for her knowledge, love and support during this difficult but natural time.

Although I had been interested in the Hospice volunteer program I didn't have a lot of self-confidence and feared that I would not be able to help someone who is dying. I tried volunteer work with a local domestic violence program but after a year became "burned out" and dissatisfied. Years went by and finally in the spring of 1994 I asked God to give me a sign of what I should do next. A couple of days later I opened the paper and came across an ad announcing the upcoming Hospice volunteer training program. Here was the "sign" I asked for. I enrolled in the program and my life was changed forever.

This book is meant to share how living with purpose can be completely rewarding, and to show the many ways Hospice provides helpful services for the patient and family.

Names of patients have been changed in consideration of privacy with the exception of my parents Margaret and Ernie, mother-in-law Olive and Mr. Peterson. He not only gave his permission for me to write about him and use his name, but made me promise that I would!

It is with the utmost respect and appreciation that I share these experiences.

❧   ☙

Section 1 –

Hospice: Discovery and Life's Purpose

My Dad's First Heart Attack

We lived in Seattle in 1962. Mom was taking my older sister Barb, 16, to the Seattle World's Fair. I had been many times so Mom decided to leave me at home with Dad.

At eight years of age, I sat on the floor playing with my Lennon Sisters paper dolls, when Dad (Ernie) walked into the room. He lay down on the couch and said, "I'm not feeling too good, Teense." (That was one of his nick names for me.) A couple of minutes later I heard him making a funny noise. I looked up. He was gasping for breath and his lips were purple. Horrified and frightened I rushed to his side. In a raspy whisper he managed to say, "I can't breathe. Go get help." With that, he closed his eyes.

I responded "Ok, Daddy!" and frantically rushed out the front door letting the screen door slam behind me. As I ran up the sidewalk, I tripped, putting my hands out to brace for my fall. Instead of hitting the ground, something lifted me upright. It wasn't anything I could see. I felt someone holding me. Then I clearly heard in my head, "Don't worry, your Daddy will be ok." Immediately a peace came over me, removing the fear and panic.

My neighbor was watering his lawn. I yelled, "Help, Bud! Daddy can't breathe and his lips are purple!"

Bud put down the hose and said, "Get Lloyd, and ask Molly to call for help." Lloyd is Bud and Molly's son. As I yelled for Lloyd, he came out of the house, Molly was right behind him.

"Lloyd, my Daddy can't breathe and Bud said for you to go to my house and help him." I was no longer panicked. Lloyd nodded and ran toward my house.

Molly took my hand, leading me into her house. She went to the phone and called for help. (There was no 911 in those days!) She sat down in her favorite chair where a cigarette burned in the ashtray. Molly pulled me onto her lap. She always chewed gum when she smoked. I could smell the combination of peppermint and tobacco on her breath. She put her cigarette out, leaned back, and said, "It will be ok, the . . ."

Before Molly could finish her sentence we heard the sirens of the fire department and ambulance. She hugged me close and put her hands over my ears, trying to block out the sound of the sirens. I pulled away and said, "Oh good, now Daddy is safe. They are here!"

I got up off Molly's lap and sat on the couch, until Bud and Lloyd came in. Bud sat next to me and told me that they were going to take my dad to the hospital to be examined. They said he was going to be okay. Bud asked me where my Mom and Barb were.

"They went to the World's Fair," I explained.

There was a knock on the door and Bud went to answer it. One of the firemen asked to speak to me. Bud brought him into the living room. He kneeled down so we were eye level and said, "Chris on behalf of the Seattle Fire Department, I want to give you this pin of bravery for helping your Dad."

After a long pause while I looked at him, a smile slowly broke my stare. "Thank you, but God told me what to do."

The firemen's eyes filled up with tears that came down his face. "How beautiful." he said.

I wasn't sure what to say or do so I smiled at him. He stood up, smiled at me and said, "Thank you for telling me that, it gives me great hope." With that he added, "Good-bye."

Molly and I hugged. "Chris, I am so proud of you." She said. "You are a very special girl full of love for others."

Bud had left a note on the kitchen counter for my Mom. It said for her to not worry, that I was at their house and to come there as soon as she got home. She did come and Bud and Molly told her what happened. Mom told me she was so proud of me.

We left the neighbor's house and went home. Mom went to the hospital to see how Dad was, while Barb and I stayed home.

That is how my life's purpose ~ helping others ~ began.

Observations

Often we die like we live. Therefore, if you live your life to the fullest, focusing on relationships in your life and respecting yourself and others, living with joy daily and serving others, you are likely to have a peaceful passing.

I have been a part of the team in many Hospice patients' lives and had many heart-to-heart conversations with them and not once have I had a patient say that they wish they had more money, possessions or fame. They always talked about their relationships. Often they talked about regretting not taking the time to listen to family or friends, of being so caught up in their work life, or just their life in general, and not making time to just be with someone; to be available both to talk and listen to that person.

I have also had many conversations with family members and friends of a terminally ill patient who were anxious because of unresolved issues with the patient or just felt they needed to share something and had not done so. I always encouraged them to make time to talk with that person. It will be too late to say things once the patient has passed. This can lead to the survivor feeling regret, sadness, guilt or frustration. Grief is natural but adding the pressure of not talking openly before someone dies can make the grieving process much harder.

After so many talks about the importance of relationships with people preparing to die, I have made my own personal goal. I will say everything I need to say to my family and friends and give them the opportunity to share what they need to say to me. I don't want to be at the end of my life with unresolved issues. I also don't want anyone in my life to have regrets that they didn't talk with me about an issue.

I want to share how people I know have lived and also how they have passed. The first is my Mother, Margaret. She was a very loving and fun person and a great friend to many. She was very involved in our church, serving as treasurer for many years and as a member of the choir. She laughed often, setting an example for me to love and laugh daily. She cared what her family and friends were thinking, feeling and doing from day to day. She always had time to be there for others. If someone needed something and she was able to help, she would. She was a team player throughout her life, and a sounding board to many.

My Mom and I had many conversations about death and the dying process and we made an agreement that when she was ready to let go, she would tell me. One day near the end of

February 2007 I called her to tell her the exciting news that she was going to be a great-grandma.

After a brief silence she said, "Oh, when is the baby due?"

I responded, "October 4th."

Again, brief silence and then she said, "Sorry honey, but that is too long for me to wait."

Naturally it was shocking for me to hear that. After taking a deep cleansing breath I said, "Mom, what do you mean?"

She replied, "I'm tired of all of the medical things that continue to happen. First I have diverticulitis to deal with. Then I fell twice, injuring my back each time. Now I have to use a walker which I hate! Then my diagnosis of early stages of colon cancer, I am not happy. I am 89 years old and don't want to be 90. I am not interested in traveling much anymore and I don't even enjoy reading like I used to."

Not sure how to respond, I finally said, "Well okay Mom. Dave and I are going on a cruise next week, and we will be gone for a week. I will call you when we get back so that we can talk more about this, ok?"

"Sure that will be fine, Honey." She replied.

Hanging up the phone I sat in a state of sadness. I knew in my logical mind that this day would come but my heart wasn't ready yet! Knowing that no time would be a good time for her to die in my eyes; I had to focus on her desires. I had made that promise when I first started my Hospice volunteer work.

Shortly after that phone call ended my husband Dave entered the room. I shared with him what Mom had said and he was shocked. We talked about it and what it could mean and both of us felt a sense of loss.

We went on our cruise, leaving our cell phones in the glove box of our car. Once back to our car I pulled my cell phone out and turned it on. Much to my surprise I had three voicemails from my sister-in-law sharing that my Mom's second husband was in the hospital with kidney failure, the result of a bad case of flu. My Mom was at her apartment in the residential community where they lived. However she too had the flu and was not doing well. My heart sank.

We lived in Arizona and Mom was in Washington State and I knew I needed to go visit her. I called my sister-in-law back to tell her we had been out of the country and asked what was happening. She was happy that I called and was honest enough to ask me to come take care of my Mom. I left two days later for a ten day stay with Mom. She got better quickly once I was there and her husband recovered and came home from the hospital a couple of days before I headed back to Arizona. It was obvious to me that I needed to be in the area to help Mom. So once home I had a talk with Dave, and we started a new adventure.

We purchased a used Motor Home, got a job as campground hosts within a 45 minute drive from my Mom and settled in. Mom continued to have one medical challenge after another over the next couple of months and finally ended up in an assisted living apartment. She told me that she would love to have me stay with her when it was her time to die. I told her I would be honored to do so. We shared our "plan" with the staff and our family and I hoped it would be a long time before she made that decision.

On September 11, 2007 the nurse from the retirement home called me to say that Mom had taken a turn for the worse and wouldn't get out of bed. I told her that I would talk to Mom and come if necessary. I called Mom's apartment and talked to her. It was obvious she was ready for me to move in with her. As I packed and prepared to move in with her, I realized she would want this to be a celebration of her life and a joyful time rather than a dreaded, sad time.

Arriving at Mom's apartment I sat down and asked her to share her exact desires with me. She stated she no longer wanted to take her medications nor eat. She was ready to sign up with Hospice, which I arranged for her immediately. She also said she wanted everyone to come see her so she could say good-bye to them while she was doing well. She told me the people she wanted to see and I made a list. I called each person and told them.

We spent the next week enjoying family and friends as they came to visit and tell her good-bye. There was a lot of laughter, some tears and we could feel love in the air. She had a great time with each visitor right through her visit with her step-grandson. He completed the people on her list.

Not long after he left she started to feel some discomfort and became a little panicky. I told the nurse and she started Mom on liquid morphine to ease the physical, emotional and mental discomfort. That helped her immediately and she started sleeping more and became quieter in general.

Saturday evening she stopped responding and was in a coma until Monday morning when she passed away peacefully. What a comfort it was to me and my entire family knowing that she was able to have the joyous celebration of her life and relationships and pass with dignity in the comfort of her own apartment.

Another example I have is of a patient named Ralph, who lived a tough life. From an early age he had to fend for himself and thus he was a very controlling and, often, an angry man. When he married he treated his wife as a possession and ordered her around. She was obedient to him but not happy. She told family members that she felt he took her voice from her. Her opinions and ideas were not valued by him. He valued money over relationships and bragged about how he was a self-made millionaire. That was first and foremost in his mind. He thought everyone shared his value of money.

When his wife became terminally ill he didn't show her compassion. He was angry that he had to take care of her. He complained to anyone that would listen that it was a horrible burden on him. Everything was always about him. He was arrogant, opinionated and judgmental. When she passed away he found himself very lonely. He had alienated most of his family and the few friends he had.

Years later he was injured in a fall and admitted to the hospital. There were complications during his operation and they had to perform a tracheotomy on his throat so he could breathe. Ironically, he also lost his voice, much as he had "taken his wife's voice" years before. He didn't have many visitors. He never recovered from that surgery. It really hit me when I realized that he died the way he lived. I found it very sad and thought about the contrast between his life and passing and how my Mom passed.

I tend to analyze things and I began thinking about the various Hospice patients I'd been assigned and the way they passed.

Continuing this thought process, I realized how important it was that I had been involved with many patients at the end of their lives and was able to help facilitate their making amends with family and friends so they had closure with everyone before passing. That is what I find so rewarding about my volunteer work.

I also learned that some people don't have the desire to make those amends and are just fine with passing with unfinished business. Although it is hard for me to understand, I also respect those people.

One of my dear friends was a very private person. She was independent and proud. She wasn't open to having others help her very often. Her relationship with her immediate family was strained. Her youngest daughter was at odds with her. Neither one of them wanted to talk it out. They just accepted that they didn't have a close loving relationship. She didn't want to depend on her adult children for her care. We talked on the phone about the services that Hospice would provide for her and she finally signed up with her local Hospice. Although she took advantage of some of the services; nurse, social worker, chaplain and case manager visits when she was in the end stages of cancer, when she got to the point where she could no longer bathe herself she called me to talk. She was upset because she didn't have the energy to take a shower. When I suggested that she allow the Hospice CNA (Certified Nurse Assistant) caregivers bathe her, she got very upset. She didn't want anyone bathing her! At a loss for how to help her I gently said, "Well, you really only have a few choices. Go without a shower, allow the Hospice team to help you, or let go and die."

After a short pause she cheerfully said, "Wow, thanks for helping me Chris. I love you." With that we said, "good-bye."

Hanging up the phone I thought maybe she would call for help. Instead, three days later her daughter called me to tell me she had passed away. I was shocked on one hand, but when I thought it through, I knew she just had too much pride and was too stubborn to allow others to help in her personal care. I felt guilty for awhile but after talking with other volunteers at our monthly meeting and also talking with the Chaplains at Hospice,

I realized she had made the choice of one of the options I had suggested.

These are only a few examples of what I have witnessed. I now pay close attention to my relationships and do my best to tell family and friends how much I love them and appreciate having them in my life. I find peace in living this way.

Awareness

My Hospice Volunteer training was an amazing journey through self. I spent 40 hours of class and many hours of processing time at home. What a gift this was for me. I thought I was going to do this work to help others, but had no idea how much I was helping myself.

Although I felt a calling to this work, I was concerned after the first training class that I would not be able to do a good job. It was very intense, involving digging down deep within me to understand just why I was so drawn to this work. Doing the different emotional exercises, in addition to learning the mechanics of how to care for a patient gave me great insight. Serving others at a time when so many changes are going on in their lives and assisting them to the best of my ability to have a peaceful, pain free journey with dignity was what fulfilled me.

I found the "loss sensitivity exercise" to be the most profound experience. We did this in the chapel, seated in a circle of chairs. Boxes of Kleenex were available between chairs that every student could easily reach if needed. We were handed 25 pieces of paper, in five different colors. Each color represented something. For instance, blue was for relationships. Yellow was for activities you enjoy doing. We wrote down the top five for each category. Once everyone was finished, the volunteer coordinator told us she was going to read us a story. It was about us becoming ill. At different places in the story she would stop reading and instruct us to toss one of our papers into the middle of the circle. It was up to each student to decide what to let go of when she instructed us. It is amazing how much I thought about why I should let each possession, experience or relationship go.

What I learned about myself during this exercise was shocking. One revelation was that the woman I thought was my best friend at the time was the paper I tossed first and easily. I was surprised I picked that to let go, rather than my joy of reading! Thinking about it, I realized that other people in my life had labeled her my best friend. I hadn't. I was willing to allow others to make that decision for me and I just went along with it. What a dishonor that was to both of us, not to mention the other great friends I had in my life!

For a couple of weeks after that class I continued to process everything I learned. It left me with personal awareness that was so valuable and that awareness changed my life forever. It gave me true insight on how a patient feels during the process of dying. They give up independence, one aspect or activity at a time, becoming more and more dependent on others. This often brings resentment and depression.

I am forever grateful to the people who presented that class for assisting me in being prepared to do such important work. This training program gave me insight and many tools to assist me during each assignment I would have for years to come. Naturally, I learned more with each patient and circumstance I was engaged with as I did my volunteer work.

My volunteer work for the hospice in California has been the most profound for me so far. The schedule we had was very supportive. Once a month we had a meeting that included continuing education and a time for talking about our "assignments." That was a huge part of self-care for me. It was mandatory to attend six of the twelve meetings. I went to almost all the meetings; being a part of a team really helped me.

My passion for the work I do is obvious to everyone around me. I have been told many times when I speak of it my entire face lights up. It is my dream to let the general public know the value of having hospice for the patient, the family and friends. There are many services available. If you are interested in doing volunteer work you will have an amazing opportunity to assist others while filling your spirit as well! If you are feeling this may be a service you would like to be involved in, please call your local hospice.

Section 2 –

My Patients' Stories

June

My first patient support assignment was for a 78 year old woman named June. She lived in the basement apartment of her daughter Betty's large home in a beautiful wooded area.

June was in Hospice because she was having complications from Multiple Sclerosis. She was very weak and had lost interest in living. The request was for a volunteer to come once a week, for four hours to sit with June while her daughter ran errands.

As I dialed the phone number to set up my first appointment my heart raced and my hands were a little shaky. Betty answered on the fifth ring. I nervously identified myself and asked her when would be a good time for me to visit with June and was there anything in particular she wanted me to do. She said June wanted to be read to from the books Betty made available. We settled on Wednesday afternoon for my first visit. The wait seemed like an eternity. Over the next five days my excitement continued to build and by Wednesday morning I was more than eager to go.

On my drive to June's house many things ran through my mind. Would June like me? Would I do a good job? What would the book that she had picked out be about? Would it be interesting to me?

Once I arrived at their home and parked my car, a peace came over me. I took a deep breath, slowly got out of my car and walked to the front door. Betty answered offering a half smile and I noticed puffy dark circles under her eyes. She welcomed me to their home and asked me to take a seat in the living room so we could chat a bit before she took me downstairs to meet June.

Insecurity began to overwhelm me as Betty spoke of her expectations for my visits. In addition to June wanting me to read to her, Betty wanted me to encourage June to walk for at least a half hour each visit. June had not been interested in much of anything and every time Betty asked her to walk June refused. Betty was hoping I could get June to walk.

She went on to say she put a stack of books on the coffee table in June's room for us to choose from. She said June needed to be stimulated and she thought history books would help. Immediately my stomach began churning. History was one of my least favorite subjects in school! I wondered if this was the best assignment for me.

As we walked down the stairs heading to June's apartment I remembered my volunteer coordinators' guidance.

"Go into each assignment with an open mind and no expectations."

As I entered June's apartment, my eyes could not process everything at once. There she was, in her silk gown, lying on her lounge chair straight out of the 1930's movies. The room was filled with many floral arrangements that made it smell wonderful. As I looked around at the many cards she received, the pictures and knick-knacks, I felt more relaxed.

June smiled up at me from her lounge chair extending her hand to shake mine in welcome. She asked me to sit in the chair close to the head of the lounge and make myself comfortable. As I sat down she turned her head to Betty and said, "Good-bye Betty. Have a great time out."

With that, Betty said good-bye and reminded me that her cell phone number was on the kitchen table upstairs if I needed her for anything while she was away.

June and I chatted a few minutes while Betty got ready and left the house. As soon as June heard Betty's car engine start she said, "Chris, please read the titles of the books Betty left to pick from." As I read the titles June said, "Oh no, these won't do. Did you bring any romance novels by chance?"

A bit stunned, I responded, "Well let me go check my car, I recently went to the used book store and I may have the bag of books still in the trunk."

As I walked to my car I hoped the bag was still there because I couldn't imagine reading any of the books Betty set out. I would be bored to death! Once I opened the trunk my worry disappeared. There sat the bag of books, including a variety of romance novels.

Back in the apartment I told June the good news and read off the titles. She picked a novel by "Danielle Steele". I sat down and began to read.

I read for about an hour and noticed that June's eyes had closed. I wondered if I should stop reading and allow her to nap awhile. I was quiet for a minute or so and she opened one eye, looking right at me and said, "Please continue Chris I can hear you with my eyes closed!"

I relaxed, and began enjoying the story myself until I reached the first love scene. It hit me then that I would be reading this out loud to a 78 year old woman. What would she think? Would she be offended? Since her eyes were closed again and I could hear her steady breathing, I decided I'd try skipping over that part but once again June opened one eye and said, "Chris, don't skip those scenes. That's what I've been waiting to hear!" I laughed and went back to reading the steamy romance until Betty returned home.

She came down to June's apartment to check in on us and found us laughing. She gave a small smile and said, "It appears you two are enjoying each other." She went on to say "Mom, how do you like the selection of books I left for you?" I looked at June and then back to Betty and once again June and I burst out laughing.

June replied, "Well dear, they were a bit dry but fortunately Chris had some books in her car so she's reading a delightful romance novel to me." Betty's slight smile disappeared into a frown. She turned and glared at me. I could feel my stomach churn and twist with the fear of not handling things correctly.

As Betty continued to frown at me and June, I wasn't sure what to do. Deciding I had to take a stand for June, I said to Betty, "Well I am here to visit with June and this is her time to do what she wants, so I felt it best to honor her request and read a book she is interested in." The room was silent as I waited for a response.

June spoke up, saying, "Betty, I appreciate you making a home for me and taking such great care of me but this is my life and I don't give a damn about any of those books you placed on the table. Although you made many great choices for me, this is one area where I can make my own decisions and it doesn't concern you!"

Betty backed up a couple of steps towards the door, a strained look on her face and said, "Yes, you are right Mother. I apologize to both of you." With that she turned and marched out of June's apartment.

When Betty was out of sight, I turned to June. Our eyes met, and we both cracked up laughing again. What a wonderful bonding experience.

As I drove home that afternoon, I was struck with a variety of emotions. First, I felt relief that my first visit was over and I knew that I had made a big difference in June's life, if only for those four hours! Secondly, I was excited that I had pushed through my fear of confrontation and stood my ground for June and ultimately for myself. It set a wonderful foundation for future visits.

I enjoyed my weekly visits with June and was thrilled when she told me what a difference I was making. She told me how much she enjoyed our time together and laughing so much.

During one visit June asked if we could talk rather than have me read to her. I settled in the chair at the head of her lounge and smiled at her. June began, "Chris, my relationship with Betty is very strained. She has resentments that go back to her childhood and I have done everything I can to try to reconcile but Betty remains angry. You see, my husband Ed had pneumonia but we didn't know it. He thought he had a bad cold. His lungs filled with fluid and he died in his sleep. It was a shock for both Betty and me. She blames me for Ed's death which has made everything worse."

With that, June began crying softly. I extended my hand and she took it in hers. We sat quietly giving her time to recover. She looked at me, eyes full of pain and said, "I had no idea he was that sick or I would have called for help." She sighed and became quiet. I continued to hold her hand and remained silent.

After a long pause June said, "When I became ill, Betty told me that she wasn't sure she was willing to help me because I didn't help her father. I was so shocked and hurt she would think that. I just sat there looking at her and couldn't talk." June continued, "Betty also told me she always resented the time I spent with her father and not with her. From a young age she felt I loved Ed more than I did her. She said she'd think about opening her home to me in my time of need but wouldn't make any promises. I am grateful that she did allow me to move in with her but she remains very angry and distant."

As we sat quietly for a few minutes I thought, *"Well, this explains the interaction between June and Betty"*. June released my hand and sat up on the lounge. She turned to me. This time she had a smile on her face and a twinkle back in her eyes. She said, "Thank you. I appreciate that I can talk to you about how I'm feeling without worrying about being judged. I feel so much better talking about this."

I smiled at June and said, "It's my pleasure June, I'm honored you feel comfortable sharing with me." That was the first of many heart-to-heart conversations we had together. June shared stories of her married life and how much she missed her husband. They enjoyed the simple things in life, like flying a kite, having a picnic and going to the movies. She told me the lounge chair was a birthday gift to her from Ed. He told her that she was his heroine and wanted her to relax in style. She was sad that Ed died at a young age, missing out on being there to watch Betty grow from a young teen into a successful woman.

She continued by sharing that she didn't see any real reason to live now that Ed was gone and she was having so many medical problems. Because Betty was angry with her so much of the time and they didn't enjoy time together, she didn't think that Betty would care if she passed.

We sat in silence once again and several things ran through my mind to share with June but from my recent hospice indoctrination I knew it was not the time to speak up. Instead I waited a few minutes and then June said, "Oh! I feel better now, thank you for listening."

"You're welcome June. Would you mind if I shared my thoughts with you?" It's very important to ask permission to share your opinions and experiences because you are there for the patient, or a family member who has asked you to listen to them. This journey isn't about the volunteer, but about the patient and the family unit. June said yes, she wanted me to share my thoughts.

"June, I want you to know I believe you have a reason for living. I think Betty needs you now more than ever. Maybe it's time to talk about Ed's passing and how it affected each of you."

To that June responded, "Well I doubt it would do any good to try to talk with Betty, I don't think it will make any difference."

"Sometimes, opening the lines of communication can lead to a much needed conversation that clears the air. If you can tell her how much you love her and that you didn't pick Ed over her, but love them both, it is possible she will be more responsive." I encouraged her to talk with her hospice social worker and ask for assistance to talk to Betty.

June sat up straight then and said, "Oh great idea! I will do that! Thank you for that insight. I hadn't thought about that. I'll call my social worker this afternoon!"

I left June's home that day feeling a great sense of accomplishment. Not only had I listened to her and honored her wishes, but I was able to give her helpful advice. It felt good to have made a difference.

June did call the social worker assigned to her and set up a meeting. June and Betty were able to talk things out with the social worker present to assist them. They worked out their differences and enjoyed making up for lost time.

Although most Hospice patients die, June got better. She recovered enough that she was able to return to her own apartment and was released from the Hospice program.

As I filled out my volunteer notes for the last visit I had with June, a variety of emotions rushed through me. Sadness that I would no longer be visiting her on a weekly basis, and happiness that her health had improved so much she was no longer in need of the Hospice program. I was also humbled and uplifted by the entire experience. June had opened her home and her personal life to me. She trusted me enough to share her most intimate thoughts and regrets.

At the next volunteer monthly meeting I happily reported to the group that June had graduated from Hospice and I was filled with gratitude to have been a part of her journey.

James

One Tuesday just as I was heading out the door the phone rang. Following my gut feeling that this was an important call, I answered the phone and was greeted by a calm yet concerned voice, "Is Christina there?"

"This is she," I said.

"Hi, Christina, this is Linda from Hospice Center, and we have a patient here requesting that you come help him. He needs to be admitted to the center but is fighting both his wife and the doctor. He said 'They' told him to have the staff call you to help solve this problem."

"I don't know this person."

After a short pause, Linda said "Christina, he seems to know you. He described you to me and said that he was sure you would come." She continued, "Since I haven't met you, I will share with you what James said. He said you have long brownish red hair, are tall, wear either contacts or glasses. When I asked him how he knew you, or knew what you looked like, he said, "I already told you, *'They'* told me!"

I stood there, stunned. "He has described me." I said. "I am not sure what is happening but I am just now heading out the door to get my hair cut. I will get this done as quickly as possible, and then drive right to the center."

Linda replied "Oh, wonderful . . . thank you so much Christina. By the way, he is very angry and uncooperative and somewhat hard to deal with, very impatient. I want you to know what to expect."

I thought a moment and responded, "Well, maybe he is just scared. At any rate, please tell him what I'm doing and I will be there as soon as I can."

"Thank you again. I will tell him!" Linda said.

As I rushed to the hair salon I could not help but wonder just who 'They' could be. My gut told me, "angels," but I was just not sure.

Arriving at the center I parked my car and sat there a minute to settle myself. I took several deep breaths and closed my eyes to calm myself and focus on the task ahead. After calming down I went inside the center to the nurse's station to check in. Approaching the nurse at the desk, I said, "Linda?"

She turned around, her eyes taking me in and then resting on my Hospice nametag. She smiled, shook my hand and said, "Hi Christina, thanks for coming. Let me explain briefly what the situation is here and then I will take you to James's room."

"Ok, that's great," I responded.

Linda explained as we walked, "James has only a matter of days to live. His family and doctors feel it best to have him admitted here to keep him as comfortable as possible. His children do not want him to die in the family home. They feel it will be too sad to live there after he passes. He wants to be home and in his waterbed. It is a sad and tough situation but at this point someone needs to get him to at least listen to why he needs to be here."

As I stood there listening to this, I thought, *"How in the world am I going to help this patient and his family?"*

Linda took me into his room. He sat slouched on the love seat, half asleep, but refusing to get into the hospital bed supplied. The rooms were designed to accommodate family members as well and included a bay window seat that was also a bed.

Linda said, "James, I have someone here to introduce you to."

With his eyes still closed James smiled and said, "Hi Christina, 'They' told me you would be here soon. Thanks for coming." With that he opened his eyes and extended his hand to shake mine. I reached out to his and shook it. "Hello James, it is nice to meet you. Although I have not met you before, you seem to know something about me, and I was wondering who 'They' are?"

At this, James smiled and said, "You know Christina, you know!" That was all he would add. Linda excused herself and left me standing there.

I walked across the room to the window seat and sat down facing him. He was still slouched on the love seat, just looking at me. My mind was racing because I knew that everyone was hoping that I could get him to lie down in the bed, and to agree to move into the center. He sat quietly watching me, waiting for my first move.

I squared my shoulders, smiled and said, "James, you don't look comfortable and you are in danger of slipping right off of that love seat. Would you consider getting in the bed?"

"I don't want to get in that bed!" James retorted.

I sat looking at him for a moment and then softly asked, "Why don't you want to get in that bed James?" I pointed to the hospital bed.

As feeble as he appeared, his voice was strong and his words clear. He angrily replied, "Because I will die there, Christina!"

Stunned, I replied, "Well would you like to lie down here on the bay window seat, and maybe take a nap with the sun on your back?"

It was the right offer. James smiled at me and said, "Yes, Christina I would like that very much."

"Great, let me help you," I said as I walked toward him. I knew this was going to be a challenge because his illness and the drugs he had to take for it created an extreme bloating in his stomach that unbalanced him. He also had trouble walking, as the circulation in his legs and feet was poor. As I took his arm and he slowly stood, I knew this was going to be a long walk for us. I realized I needed to stand behind James and assist him that way to help keep him balanced. I stepped behind him placing my right hand in the small of his back. With my left hand, I supported his left elbow to guide him to the bay window bed.

We took a few steps and he was so tired that he seemed to drift off to sleep. He started to fall back against me and I knew we were in trouble. I am not sure if I just thought the words in my head, or if I said them out loud but this is what I said, "Angels, please help us, or we are going to fall to the floor!"

Instantly I felt a gentle pressure on the small of my back, and another between my shoulder blades creating a comforting warm spot. We safely glided across the floor to the window seat.

I helped James lie down. Shortly after that he drifted off to a peaceful sleep.

He rested a while, and then began to stir. Without opening his eyes he began to talk to me. "Christina, I had a very full life and there are things I am not proud of. There is something concerning me and I am not sure if you can help with it or not. Although both my wife Cathy and I grew up Catholic, I left the church and do not wish to have a Catholic funeral. Cathy has remained very involved in the church and hinted that she will find comfort in having a proper Catholic funeral for me. It upsets me to think of that happening. I don't want to bring this up because I know it will cause a confrontation and I don't want to use the little energy I have, fighting with my wife and have that be a lasting memory for her once I have passed on." He stopped talking then because we both heard someone approaching.

His wife, Cathy, walked into the room. She stopped. Looked at us . . . looked back to the love seat where she had last seen her husband slumped and angry. "Oh my, oh my!" Cathy said, "Thank you for convincing James to lie on the window seat."

Cathy approached James who was now looking at her. She tenderly kneeled down in front of him and said, "James, honey, we just finished talking with everyone and you are going to have to stay here. I cannot take you back home. I am sorry." Tears began to roll down her cheeks and James began to protest but, noticing her tears, he took a deep breath and stopped in mid sentence.

James was quiet - we all were - as Cathy gently stroked his face and looked at him with sad, pleading eyes. After a short time he said, "Ok honey, I will stay here." Immediately, we were all relieved. Even James seemed to relax.

Together Cathy and I assisted him into the hospital bed. Once he was safely in the bed and comfortable, I prepared to leave. At that time I thought my work was done. However, it soon became apparent that my work was just beginning!

Linda entered the room, touched Cathy's arm, and spoke softly to her. Cathy looked at Linda and nodded her head. At that point Linda released Cathy's arm and approached James' bedside. She stopped, turned to me and said, "Christina, would you have time to go out for a short walk with Cathy in the Rose Garden while I get James settled in here?"

Looking at my watch to check the time I then looked at Linda, then to Cathy, and back again to Linda. "Yes, I have time to take a walk with Cathy." I turned to James. "Rest well James and we will be back soon."

As I started to walk from the room, he called out, "Ok, Christina, and thank you!"

"You are very welcome," I said over my shoulder as Cathy and I headed out of the room.

As we walked in silence, we headed to the path that leads to the Rose Garden. We were each lost in our own thoughts as we walked, feeling comfortable just being together.

Approaching a bench Cathy asked if we could sit down. I joined her on the bench. The sun shone down on us, and we were surrounded by beautiful roses and other flowers.

Cathy looked at me, "Christina, I am not positive how you ended up here to help us, but James kept saying 'They' told him to ask for you. We have never met before, and you obviously look just like he described you. He seems to *know* you are the volunteer for us. I am going to accept this as truth because no one else could get him to lie on a bed, but it did not take you very long. That in itself was amazing and I am so grateful to you. It's easy to see the connection you have with him." As we sat there Cathy continued talking. She was concerned at how angry James seemed to be.

I began to understand some of what he had told me. As she shared some of his mood swings and the things that he said and did, I quickly understood that he had issues that were keeping him from allowing the process of passing on. At that moment I realized I needed to talk to the Chaplain and the nurse to tell them the information that James told me. I suggested to Cathy that we go inside; that I had some things to share with the Hospice staff that I thought would help with James' frustrations.

She and I went into the center. As we entered the kitchen on James' pod, Irene, the Chaplain came into the room. Stunned for a moment, I said, "Irene, I was just thinking I needed to talk to you and here you are!"

She smiled and said, "How may I help you?"

Irene and I went into her office and I briefly shared James' concern about Cathy preparing a Catholic funeral. She thanked me for the information and said she would take care of it.

Leaving the center I thought about the amazing chain of events that got me involved in this critical situation. As I drove home I thanked God for guiding me and asked that James' passing be peaceful.

A couple of days later I went to the center to drop off some paperwork and decided to stop in and see James. Cathy was getting him into the wheelchair when I knocked on his door. As I entered they both smiled and said, "Hi Christina. We were just talking about you! James wants to go for a ride in the Rose Garden. Would you like to join us?"

"Sure. Let's go!" With laughter, we headed outside.

It was a beautiful spring day and James seemed thrilled to be out in the fresh air. As I walked next to the wheelchair he reached out and took my hand in his. He squeezed it tenderly. Looking up at me, his eyes filled with tears, "Christina I am so thankful for your assistance. You have helped me and my family more than you will ever know."

I smiled back at him, tears slowly rolling down my cheeks and answered, "You are most welcome. It is my honor."

Cathy parked the wheelchair next to a bench and she and I sat down together. James took a deep breath and said, "Isn't it beautiful out today? The roses smell wonderful!" Cathy and I agreed. We sat in silence for about 15 minutes, enjoying the birds singing and the many flowers and plants.

James was ready to go back to his room, so we headed to the patio entrance on the opposite side of the building from where we came out. As we approached the entrance, Cathy and I realized we faced a challenge. A path of grass and stones led to the sidewalk in front of the doors. It was not a path designed for wheelchairs. On the right side was a beautiful fish pond. Lily pads floated and large gold fish swam below the surface. We paused trying to figure out the best approach to get James across the path. We asked him to hold on tight. He laughed, saying, "Ok girls I'm ready!"

Cathy stayed at the back of the wheelchair to push and I went to the front, bending down to grab the foot rests and help pull the wheelchair onto each stone. We did fine on the first couple of stones but when we tried the next stone the wheelchair just stopped. Determined to get him to the sidewalk I said, "Let's try again Cathy, this time I will try to pull harder."

James giggled as I took my stance and pulled with all my might. I pulled a little too hard and the wheelchair went right up the stone, I fell backwards . . . dipping my head right into the pond. As soon as my head hit the water I burst out laughing. By this time James was laughing hard and Cathy was squealing with delight!

Other people in the area looked at us, and began laughing too. Just then a visiting doctor came to my rescue and helped get James and his wheelchair over the last couple of stones to safety.

Once back in his room, James continued to smile. He was visibly tired and moved slowly getting into the bed. Looking at me and my dripping wet hair he started laughing again. That set me off laughing again as well. Exhausted, we both got quiet. He said, "Christina, you are so much fun. I really needed to laugh, and what an angel you have been. For the first time in years, I am totally at peace. I have no more fear. Instead, I am full of joy. You are a large part of the reason for that. Once again, thank you."

Not knowing what to say, I went to his side, leaned into him, allowing my soggy fish pond soaked hair to brush his face, I kissed his forehead, squeezed his hand, "I, too, am filled with joy, my friend." We smiled at each other. I released his hand, turned and began to walk out of the room. As I reached the door I turned for one last look. James was already drifting off to sleep with a smile on his face.

The next afternoon I had errands to run and when I returned home I saw that a message blinked on our answering machine. Playing the message, my heart squeezed tight and began to beat faster, "Christina, this is Linda from Hospice, please call us as soon as you get in, this is regarding James." I knew then my new friend had passed on.

With trembling fingers I managed to dial the number. Linda answered on the third ring. Gently she confirmed what I already knew: James had passed away peacefully that morning. His family asked that Linda thank me again for being a big part of making his last few days on this earth bearable and allowing him to keep his dignity. His last wishes were met and although we will all miss him, his spirit lives on with all of us!

Bert

Bert was a resident of the Hospice center. He was 43 years old and had been a very active member of a local Harley Davidson Motorcycle club. He had cancer and had recently deteriorated to the point of needing full time care. He didn't want to die in his home all alone and didn't have anyone available to stay and care for him. Once he realized he could no longer take proper care of himself he initiated the process of moving into the center.

He was a tall man, over 6 feet with a larger than life presence. His strawberry blonde hair was cut short and styled perfectly. When he spoke, the air vibrated!

I met him when I went into the living room in his pod wing. He sat in an easy chair, staring straight ahead. Smiling, I said, "Hello" as I walked in.

I went to the bookcase to get a book for a patient and when I turned around to leave, Bert said, "Hi there. How are you?"

I was a bit surprised since he took a while to respond to my earlier greeting. I stopped and said, "I'm doing well, how are you?"

He looked up and said, "To tell you the truth, awful!"

"I'm sorry to hear that, if you would like to talk more I'd be happy to come back after I take this book to my patient."

Bert then said, "Sure, I'd love to complain to you!"

Laughing I said, "Okay, I'll be right back."

As I walked to my patient's room, I couldn't help thinking I was in for an interesting time when I got back to Bert. Entering Edna's room I gave her the book and she thanked me. I asked her if she needed anything more right then.

She responded, "No thanks, I'd like to start reading this book while I'm awake and feeling good."

"Okay great. I'll stop back before I leave for home."

As I returned to the living room, I noticed that Bert's eyes were closed. Quietly I headed to the couch directly across from the chair that Bert was sitting in. I sat down and waited to see if he was asleep or just resting. A moment later he opened his eyes and said with surprise in his voice, "You came back!"

"Yes of course I did. Do you still want to visit with me?"

"Yes I do. Thanks, Chris. What I want to talk about is this: how in the world did I get here? To be terminally ill and in no way prepared for my death. The choices I made put me here for the most part. I lived a fast and careless life and don't have much to show for it. Five years ago I had a beautiful girlfriend who loved me unconditionally. What did I give her in return? Heartache. I wasn't willing to open up to her and she finally had had enough and left. I haven't been in a relationship since. The real love in my life is Annie, my potbelly pig! I have friends in the motorcycle club but don't really get close to anyone or allow them to get close to me. Now I'm at the end of my life, at the age of 43, with no one to share this journey with. I'm sad and lonely. It's very hard to admit, but it's the truth."

I sat there quietly allowing Bert to process what he had just shared. During the silence I was thinking how honored I felt that Bert was comfortable enough to share such personal information with me. After a couple of minutes he smiled and said, "It really felt good to say that out loud. I didn't realize most of that until I started telling you about it. Thank you for listening to me. I feel like you cared and that you are not judging me."

"It was my pleasure Bert. Now I have a question for you. Where is Annie?"

"She's in my room" Bert responded. "I'm so happy she was allowed to move in with me. I wasn't sure they would allow a potbelly pig! I'm thrilled to have her here with me. Would you like to meet her?"

"Sure!" I said. Bert and I stood up in unison and walked to his room. As we entered, there was Annie, curled up napping on her bed. Bert whistled. Annie jumped right up and came running to him, just like a dog would. She snorted and wagged her little curly tail at Bert. Bert told her he had someone that wanted to meet her. He then turned to me and said, "Chris, this is Annie."

Bending down, I said, "Hi Annie. You are so cute!" Turning to Bert I added, "May I pet her?"

"Sure, she loves to be touched." Bert said.

Kneeling down to be closer to Annie I began petting her. I was surprised at how coarse and prickly her hair felt on my hand as I stroked her head and down her back. She seemed to enjoy my touch as I chatted to her. She looked at me as if trying to decipher what I was saying. She had the sweetest eyes and her gaze made me feel she was very comfortable with me. After a few minutes of petting her, I stood up and announced it was time for me to head home.

Bert asked me if he could have a hug. I said, "Well sure. I'd like that very much." With that, we hugged and said our good-byes and I left his room.

I went back to Edna's room and found her sound asleep on her couch with the book I had brought her lying open against her chest. I wrote her a note to tell her I had stopped in to say good-bye on my way out.

On my drive home that day, thoughts ran through my mind like a ticker tape. I hoped I had spent enough time with Edna and that she would enjoy the note I left for her. Would Bert want me to come visit him again? Would he have friends visit him on a regular basis?

I visited with Bert several times when I was in the center. Once Annie saw me she would follow me through the halls like a dog follows its master. I quickly became close to both Bert and Annie. I was so happy to see Bert did indeed have lots of friends that came to visit with him. They were all members of his motorcycle club and were loud and joyful.

Before meeting Bert and his friends I had a biased opinion of motorcycle groups. They have been presented by the media as bad guys, trouble makers, and even criminals. At first I was a bit afraid, or at the very least intimidated by this group. After observing them a few times I began to enjoy visiting with them in the common area living room.

One day Bert saw me in the hall outside his room and he called out to me. "Chris, would you come visit me when you have time?"

Looking into his room I said, "Sure, would now be a good time?"

"Oh, yes, that would be great. Come on in!" Bert replied. I entered and sat on the love seat across from his bed. Annie got off her bed and trotted to me, snorting all the way.

She put her head in my lap and nudged me. I leaned down and kissed the top of her nose, patting the top of her head at the same time. "Hi Annie girl, how are you?" I said as I continued to pet her.

Bert smiled as he watched me interact with Annie. After a few moments, he cleared his throat, "Chris I can see how much you and Annie love each other and I was wondering if when I die, you would take Annie as your pet?"

I was stunned. I didn't know what to say. "Oh Bert, what a wonderful offer, I do love Annie very much. But I have two dogs and a cat at home and I just couldn't take her."

Bert just stared at me, with a blank look on his face.

After a moment of silence I said, "Bert, I'm so sorry."

Bert cut me off saying, "I can't believe you would say no. I thought for sure you would take her and I could pass in peace knowing she would have a loving home to go to."

I waited a few minutes and said, "Bert I am sorry. I know your friends love Annie; do you think maybe one of them would take her?"

Bert continued staring at me and finally he said, "Well maybe but you were my real choice. I'll think about who to ask." With that he closed his eyes. "Thanks for stopping in, Chris; I'm going to take a nap now."

I left Bert's room feeling sad. As I walked down the hall to the front of the building I thought about how I could possibly convince my husband that it would be a good idea to adopt Annie. By the time I reached my car I realized I was only considering that because I knew that I had disappointed Bert. Right then I decided I had a right to say no. Even though it was not the answer Bert wanted to hear, I knew I couldn't adopt Annie and it wouldn't be good for her to live in a home with other pets. She needed to live in a home where she was the only pet.

Bert's health went downhill fairly quickly and he was bedridden. His friends came and took turns staying with him around the clock. One of his friends adopted Annie so Bert knew she had a loving home to go to once he passed.

I saw Bert a couple of times when I was in the center. The last time I saw him he was unresponsive. I was sad knowing that his time was near and that I wouldn't see him at the center much longer.

Three days later Bert passed peacefully with Annie lying on the foot of his bed with him! Six of his friends surrounded the bed. When he stopped breathing Annie began making a noise expressing her pain. She knew he had died. Her new adopted Mom reached for her and held her close. Annie wiggled away from her arms and jumped off the bed onto the window seat next to Bert's hospital bed. She let out another squeal, jumped to the floor and ran out of the room.

At the Hospice center there is a tradition when a patient passes and it is time for the mortuary to come and remove the body, anyone who works or is a volunteer with Hospice can escort the body from the center. A death quilt made by a volunteer group is put over the body as a special escort.

When Bert's body was ready to be taken to the morgue they made the announcement at the center that all escorts were to report to the station. I quickly walked to the station and got in line. It was truly an honor to walk with Bert to the waiting hearse along with other volunteers, staff, and Bert's friends, and of course, Annie. She walked close to the body and once again began squealing in a way that sounded like she was crying. As we approached the doorway we all stopped to watch Bert's body as it was put into the hearse. Annie stopped at the end of the hearse and made one last loud cry.

What a beautiful yet painful sight that was. Annie's new owner, Britney, attached Annie's leash and gently told her it was time to go to her new home. I stood in the doorway and watched the hearse drive off, then turned to see Britney and Annie walk down the hall towards Bert's room. It was touching to know that Annie, who gave such unconditional love to Bert, was going to have a loving home to go to.

Whispering I said, "Thank you Bert, for teaching me not to judge someone by the clothes they wear, or a group they belong to. Our time together was short but very rewarding. I hope you are at peace now and you find the love you longed for during your life here."

Olive

Olive was my mother-in-law. I met her when I was 14 years old. She nicknamed herself Mom2 and would sign cards using that signature. We weren't very close until I was in my thirties. She and her second husband, Fred (Dave's dad died shortly before I met them) moved closer to where we lived and I visited with her often. She didn't have a driver's license and began inviting me to take her to church lunch programs with the Women's Society group. It was an honor and although I was the youngest there, I enjoyed the time together. Olive and I had wonderful chats in the car coming and going to these outings.

When I began doing my Hospice volunteer work Olive asked me questions. We had several great talks about the value of being in Hospice. One day while Dave and I were visiting at Olive's home, she told me that she wanted me to be with her when it was her time to die. I told her that I would be honored to be with her. This made her happy.

Olive had several mini strokes that led to her being admitted into a nursing home. When filling out the admission paperwork it was noted that Olive wanted me to be present during her passing if at all possible.

On September 16, 1996, shortly after Dave headed out-of-town for the day with our only car, the receptionist at the nursing home called me to say that Olive had slipped into a coma and was not expected to live more than a day or two. I thanked her and told her that I would be there as soon as I could get a ride. I asked to have someone go to Olive's room and tell her that I was coming.

After I hung up the phone I was nervous and sad. Although I had a lot of training and experience, this was someone that I loved very much and knew it would be different than sitting with a patient. I decided to call my friend who is a pastor. He said a prayer with me and gave me a great pep talk. I will be forever grateful to him for that. It put me in the right frame of mind to sit with Olive.

My neighbor gave me a ride. As we pulled up to the front entrance, I got butterflies in my stomach. Taking a deep breath and releasing the nerves I hugged my friend good-bye and thanked her for the ride.

As I walked down the hall to Olive's room I was over-whelmed with joy. What an honor to be at my mother-in-laws side during this sacred time.

I stopped at the nurse's station to let them know I was there. One of the nurses that I had become friendly with warned me that Olive's body had already started to discolor. She didn't want me to be frightened when I saw her. She said that changes started about midnight the night before.

Even with the warning, when I walked into Olive's room I was stunned. She looked so tiny and frail in the hospital bed. Fred was there and got up to greet me when I entered the room. He had a chair on the far side of the bed. I pulled another chair up next to Olive on the near side. I leaned over and kissed her cheek and sat down. I took her hand into mine and was shocked to see how purple her skin was. I spoke to her knowing that hearing is the last sense that goes when someone dies.

At lunchtime I said, "Mom2, we are going to go get something to eat. It is 12:15 right now, and we will be back by 1:30. If you want to leave while we are gone that is ok. If you want us to be with you then we would be happy if you wait."

Fred and I went to lunch and talked about what it was like sitting there and waiting for her to die. He was very sad on one hand, but wanted it over. I guess I felt about the same but didn't really say that out loud. We ate and headed back to the nursing home.

Entering Olive's room I was relieved to see that she was still alive. Sitting in my chair I once again took her hand. I noticed that her breathing was shallower than earlier. I was thankful for my Hospice training because I was able to recognize different stages her body was going through.

Shortly before 6 PM, I had my left hand on her chest while holding her hand with my right; I could feel her heart beating slower and slower. She took a deep breath and I felt her heart stop. I held my breath for a moment waiting for her to take another breath and her heart to beat; neither happened. I turned my head to her husband who was watching me and said, "She's gone now." He nodded but did not speak.

We sat in silence for maybe a minute. I said, "Please get the nurse and tell her Olive has passed. They will have to come in and check her and call the time of death." He nodded again without speaking and left the room.

The nurse and CNA came rushing into the room with Olive's husband following behind them. They smiled at me as I sat in the chair, holding Olive's hand. They checked her pulse, listened for a heartbeat and confirmed what I already knew, Olive had died.

I released her hand, leaned over her body and gave her a kiss on the forehead. I told her how much we all loved her and were going to miss her. I thanked her for wanting me to be with her.

Although she was in a coma I believe she could hear me until the end. It gave me great comfort to know she was finally at peace.

Gloria

One fall morning Mary, my volunteer coordinator, called me with a new assignment. She told me this was a very complicated situation. She went on to say the family had a lot of issues that really needed to be worked through and she wanted me to think about if I was up for such a challenging assignment. I told her I would think about it over night and call her the next day.

This is what I learned: The patient's name was Gloria. She was 57 years old and had a cancerous brain tumor. She had four adult children (two male and two female) and three grandchildren. She lived with her daughter Patty. Patty's older sister, Priscilla was recently divorced and it had caused a lot of anger and fear within the family. Priscilla had a seven year old daughter, Peggy and they lived about ten miles from Gloria and Patty but didn't visit often due to the strain since the divorce. Gloria's sons lived out of state but moved in her area and rented a furnished home about six miles from her house when she was admitted to Hospice. Due to the family issues they did not come to visit often. They usually called her instead.

After some soul searching, I decided that I would accept this challenging assignment and do the best I could to help this family.

The following day I called Patty's home to introduce myself and set an appointment for my first visit. The moment Patty answered the phone I could hear the fear, fatigue and frustration in her voice. I asked if they would like me to volunteer. Her attitude changed immediately and she asked me to come as soon as possible. We set an appointment for the following morning, said our good-byes, and, as I was hanging up the phone, I heard Patty mutter to herself, "Thank God, maybe I will have some help with Mom now." Hearing that brought chills up and down my spine. I felt needed! Throughout that day Gloria and her family came to my mind off and on. What are the issues they have? Although divorce can often be a stressful and unhappy time, I was curious why it had hit this entire family so hard and caused estrangement with the siblings. There had to be more to the story, I thought. By the evening I was worried. Could I possibly help them become a loving family unit again? And would it be before Gloria passed? Realizing that I was thinking too much and creating stress when that wasn't helpful or positive, I took a few deep breaths and released the need to be fearful.

The next morning I awoke from a restless sleep, and went through my morning routine on "auto pilot" with thoughts ranging from excitement to fear going in and out of my mind. Once again I took deep breaths, calming myself and remembering that all I can do is my best effort. I had great training and experience and although each assignment is different, I'm always me. With that attitude firmly in place I went to my car and started the drive to Gloria's house.

Her home was located off a heavily traveled main road, down a beautiful gravel road surrounded by large trees. When you drive to the parking area it's as if you have entered a small forest. After parking my car I got out and took in the wonderful feeling and smell of nature. Automatically I took several deep breaths and felt calm and ready for my next adventure. What a challenge this assignment would turn out to be!

As I approached Gloria's home, I wasn't sure what door to knock on, as it was a long building with several homes attached and there appeared to be two main doors to this home. As I stood there trying to decide what door to use, I heard a car pulling into the parking area. As I looked at the car, much to my surprise out stepped Jack, the hospice social worker assigned to this family. I must admit I was offended to see him! This is very unusual for a social worker to come along on a visit with the volunteer. My first reaction was to feel insulted; worried he might think I wasn't going to do a good job. Then I realized I was reacting out of fear, so I took a deep breath and smiled at him.

He returned my smile and said, "I tried to call you earlier but you had already left. I'm here to introduce you because this is a very difficult situation and there are a lot of fear and trust issues with this family in general. I'm sorry I wasn't able to let you know my plan ahead of time." That changed my attitude and helped me to relax.

Jack guided me to the door at the far end of the home. Patty answered immediately and rushed to hug Jack. He hugged her briefly, releasing her and taking a step back. He then introduced me to Patty. She smiled warmly, shook my hand with enthusiasm and invited us in.

Entering the living room I immediately noticed how dark it was. The shades were closed keeping the beautiful sunlight out. The room was full of furniture, stuck here and there; making it appear someone had put everything there randomly. To the right was a small dining area. A table was stacked with what looked to be 75 books! Glancing further to the right against the wall at the front of the house, I saw a bookshelf that must have had 150 books. Obviously this family enjoyed reading! The books made me think of my first hospice patient June, and the fun I had reading romance novels to her, and reminded me again how much I enjoy this work. This gave me a new sense of excitement for this assignment.

Jack suggested we chat a bit before Patty introduced me to her Mom. I nodded in agreement. We followed Jack to the couch in the living room that appeared to "belong" where it was sitting. Patty and I sat on the couch and Jack pulled an ottoman over so he could sit facing us. He started the chat by saying, "Christina, Gloria is rapidly declining and is very upset and angry. She wants her family to get back to being a family and stop arguing about everything. Patty shared with me last night that she wants you to know all of the issues so you can see if you can talk to Gloria about them."

Patty looked at me with hope and fear in her eyes.

I responded, "Well, I'm open to doing what I can to assist this family. Patty, do you want to tell me what the issues are now?"

Looking down at the floor, Patty responded, "Yes, but I don't want you to be upset or leave when you hear these awful things." She looked up at me then and her eyes pleaded. They made my stomach churn.

Before I could say anything, Jack spoke up, "Patty, Christina is here to assist you. She won't judge you or anyone in your family. She is well-experienced in her work. Just share with her what's heavy on your heart."

Taking a deep breath Patty began, "Christina, my sister Priscilla just got a divorce. None of us saw it coming. She and Jake had what looked to all of us to be a great and very happy marriage. Jake is heart-broken and very depressed because Priscilla left him. None of us could make any sense out of it, and Jake would not tell us why Priscilla left. He just kept telling us to ask her. When I asked my sister she would say that it's none of our business with a warning tone in her voice. I waited a week and asked her again. I must have talked to her when she was in a good mood or something because she answered me. She said, "Well Patty, I have lived a lie for too long now. I finally came to grips with who I am. I couldn't live being dishonest to myself or Jake any longer. The truth is, Patty, I'm gay."

Patty slumped then and started crying. I looked at Jack for guidance and he just nodded his head. I cleared my throat and leaned toward Patty. She looked up at me and I smiled at her and opened my arms. She let out a huge sigh and grabbed me for a hug. I hugged her back and said, "Patty that is nothing to be ashamed of, nor does it offend me in any way."

Patty slowly released me; sitting back up straight on the couch she turned toward me and said, "Really? I'm so glad to hear that."

Jack spoke as he stood up and put the ottoman back in place, "Ladies, I'm going to leave now and let you continue to talk. Thanks so much, Christina. I'll be chatting with you soon." He headed for the door and left.

This was a good example of the importance of focusing on the family and remembering this was their journey, not mine. I shared with Patty that it wasn't a problem that would make me leave and that was all she needed to hear in that moment. I have learned to listen more and say less during these times. You can encourage a person to share what they wish by listening and not saying much of anything.

Patty continued to tell me the issues they were having as a family. She was concerned that in a few years, when she reached Priscilla's age, she may discover that she too, might be gay, since Priscilla is. She was terrified of what that would mean if she did. Gloria's sons didn't have tolerance for Priscilla either. Patty said that her brothers would not talk to Priscilla anymore and they refused to be at the same location with her. She said that she and her brothers were ashamed of Priscilla and didn't understand why she would pick that lifestyle and why she had to do it when Gloria was so ill.

I sat on the couch listening to Patty. When she became quiet and turned to look at me again, I asked her if she was ready to introduce me to Gloria. With a deep sigh she said, "OK, but look out, she's cranky and obnoxious. She likes to make people mad." As we got up, Patty said, "Mom says my brothers and I have been mean to Priscilla and we need to apologize to her. We don't think we are being mean and we basically don't want anything to do with her. So that's the main problem, but we have had problems over the years and some of those problems have been with Mom. I'll take you to her room now, and get ready to go grocery shopping while you visit with her."

As we headed down the hall to Gloria's area of the house I silently said a prayer asking for guidance to help me make a difference.

When I entered her room, the first sense that came to me was clinical. It felt impersonal and cold, like a hospital room. The contrast of her room and any of the rooms in the hospice center I worked in before was shocking to me. I wondered if Gloria would feel better with some changes in her living space.

As we got into the room I saw Gloria in her hospital bed. She was wearing a turban and a well-worn nightgown. She gave me a half smile as Patty introduced me and she sized me up and down. I could feel her cold calculating stare all the way through my body! I took a deep breath and smiled wider. I offered my hand to shake hers but she just continued staring at me. Patty started to scold her Mom but I put my hand on Patty's arm and said, "It's ok Patty, Gloria doesn't need to shake my hand if she doesn't want to."

I walked to the corner of the room to get a folding chair and set it next to Gloria's bed. Turning to Patty I said, "Thanks Patty, I'm all set so you can go do your grocery shopping now."

Patty looked at her Mom waiting for a response to her leaving. Gloria looked me over one more time and then she turned to Patty and nodded her head. With that Patty left the room to run her errands.

Gloria didn't say anything to me; she just lay in her bed with her eyes focused on the ceiling. I sat quietly, patiently waiting for her to say something. I was following her lead. After three or four minutes of silence Gloria finally said, "Well Christina, what makes you think you can help me or my family?"

"Wow, what a great way to start out" I thought to myself. I cleared my throat and responded, "Well Gloria, helping others is my passion. Right now I am helping Patty by being here with you in case you need something. She can go buy groceries so

your kitchen is stocked and she can make meals for you. If that is all I do today, it will be helping both of you."

Sitting quietly Gloria appeared to process my response. She continued to have a slight frown on her face, brow furrowed. She turned to me then. My natural instinct when someone looks at me is to smile.

When I smiled at her, she shouted, "Knock off that smiling, you don't know me and there's not a damn thing to smile about!"

That shocked me because I hadn't experienced a patient yell at me before. I just sat there and I have no idea why, but I giggled.

Gloria looked at me, eyes wide open, and an angry look on her face. She didn't say anything. She just stared at me. I held her glance and continued smiling, I couldn't help it.

After awhile she looked up at the ceiling, let out a sigh, released her frown and smiled! I continued to sit silently and wait for her next move. My thoughts were racing, *what would I do with this patient for two or three hours? How could I make her understand I was there to help, not judge her or her family?*

Lost in my own thoughts I was a bit startled when Gloria said, "How would you like to be in my position?" Before I could answer she sat up straight in her bed and pulled her turban off to expose her bald head, the effect of recent chemotherapy treatment. With anger she turned to the side of her bed, got out of bed, stood up, and pulled her nightgown off throwing it across the room! She then looked at me with such anger that it made my stomach churn. Naturally, I saw the scars from surgeries she had in the past. She was very thin and her body looked as if it was failing her.

I stood up looking her in the eye, smiling at her and said, "Gloria would you please get back into bed?" She just looked at me and sat on the side of the bed. I walked across the room to get her nightgown and brought it back to her. She reached her arms over her head and I assisted her back into her nightgown and then into her bed.

Once she was settled I said, "Okay, have I proven myself to you yet, or do you wish to continue to try and shock me?" What happened next surprised me the most!

Gloria cracked up laughing and said, "Well SHIT, I guess by your question that you figured out what I was doing so yes, you pass." We burst out laughing and our journey of friendship, love and emotional healing began!

Gloria opened up to me then. She told me of her anger at her children. She asked me if I knew what she was referring too. I told her that Hospice staff had said there were some family issues that had escalated to estrangement. I told her that during my chat with Patty she told me all about Priscilla's divorce from Jake and the reason. I then said, "How do you feel about the fact that Priscilla is gay?"

She sat quietly for a moment, deep in thought and then she said, "Thanks for asking me that question, Christina. How I feel about it is that I am glad that she is finally living her truth! I am sorry that Jake is so hurt, and my other children and grandchildren are so hurt from their divorce and her announcement. I am extremely angry and disappointed in my children for their selfish and arrogant response to Priscilla! Who do they think they are? They are not perfect and I hate to tell them but they are not better than Priscilla! Damn I'm mad at them!" With that her smile vanished and her expression returned to anger and sadness.

I sat there a minute or two and then leaned over to Gloria and offered my hand. Much to my surprise she took my hand and let out a big sigh. Looking at me, the anger in her face was gone but the sadness remained. Our eyes met and I smiled and we sat there for a few minutes holding hands in silence.

During that quiet time I realized how powerful both silence and human touch can be. There was no need for words.

Silence was what was needed. Each of us sat peacefully holding our own thoughts while feeling connected by our hands.

Gloria looked over at me releasing my hand she said, "Thank you Christina, for being here for me. Thank you for not letting me shock you or push you away. Thank you for asking me what I thought and felt. During the last four weeks no one has really asked me what I wanted for my last days here on earth."

I took that as a hint, "I'll ask you now, how do you feel about your care, surroundings and your family issues?" Sitting back in my chair, I waited as Gloria collected her thoughts to answer me.

"I want to spend the rest of my time here happy and peaceful. I want my family to snap out of this crazy war they are fighting and to have them visit me. I want the entire family, including Jake, to be here at the same time. I want to be able to talk to them about the fact that I am dying. I don't want it to be a taboo subject. They tiptoe around the fact I'm going to die. I'm likely going to die soon. I'm at peace with dying, but not until my family is back on track and loving each other unconditionally like they used to. I want the freedom to tell Priscilla that I am so very proud of her for coming out and taking charge of her life and living the truth. I want to tell my other kids to shut up and get over it! They aren't going to "catch" being gay just because their sister is! I want to tell them the reason I am so angry is because they are wasting time by trying to be right. Instead, we could spend time together laughing and loving each other. My energy is depleting quickly and the stress of this family war is making my time here shorter!" With that, she took a deep breath and closed her eyes.

I was quiet for a moment and then said, "Thank you so much for sharing that with me. Have you told all of that to Jack, the Hospice Social Worker?"

She opened her eyes and turned to look at me as she said, "No, for some reason I just haven't felt comfortable talking to him about all of this. But I would love it if you would talk to my family and tell them what I have said."

Many thoughts ran through my head. I didn't want to upset her by telling her that I had to report the information to Hospice and they would talk to the family members. The Hospice team members work together. Often the volunteer is the one that a patient or family member will share their thoughts and concerns with. However, the role of the volunteer is to report these conversations to the volunteer coordinator and write it in the progress notes, and the social worker will then be informed. Each Hospice has specific procedures. The volunteer goes through the volunteer coordinator with everything first. In this case I was comfortable reaching out to Jack since he introduced me to this family in person. What I knew I had to do next was to tell Jack about what Gloria had just shared. I wasn't sure how she would respond to hearing the information had to be given to the volunteer coordinator. So I just said, "I'll see what I can do to get your information to your family members." She nodded in response and closed her eyes. With that I rose and left the room.

I went to the living room and sat down to start writing my progress notes. About ten minutes later Patty returned home. I offered to help her bring the groceries in from the car. Without hesitation, she accepted my offer. Once we finished unloading, Patty began putting the groceries away. She asked me how my visit went and I told her it went very well.

Sensing that Patty was going to ask me what Gloria and I talked about, I decided it was a good time for me to leave. Picking up my purse and notebook I said, "I'm going to leave now Patty. Thank you for allowing me to stay with your Mom. It was nice meeting you both and I look forward to visiting again next week."

Patty stopped what she was doing and rushed to me as I reached the front door. She said, "Thank you so much Christina. I can't tell you how nice it is to have you on the team. I look

forward to getting to know you better. Have a great day!"
Smiling, I headed out the door.

Once in my car I took a deep breath and released it. That
helps me clear my thoughts from the time spent with patients and
brings me back to focusing on my life. Driving home I felt a
sense of accomplishment.

When I got home I finished filling out my progress report
and called the Hospice office. Jack was not in so I decided to talk
with the volunteer coordinator, Mary. She asked me to fax my
progress notes to her to make it easier to pass along the
information to Jack. She thanked me for all of my efforts and
assured me that she would get in touch with Jack as soon as
possible.

The next week when I visited Gloria she was very happy.
She had great color in her cheeks and greeted me with a huge
smile, saying, "Hi Christina! It's great to see you. I have missed
you since your last visit. Thank you so much for your help. Jack
came by and we had a talk and I basically told him what I told
you. He was very supportive. That surprised me for some reason.
He called a family meeting and we are now working together to
overcome the issues facing us. It gives me a great sense of relief,
knowing that we will be able to be a family again. That we will
spend time laughing and just being us. Jake and I visited

privately and he is now getting counseling to help process the loss of his marriage and to assist him in forgiving Priscilla. His goal is to co-parent with Priscilla peacefully and lovingly. I can now pass in peace!"

"I'm so happy to hear that. Great!" I said. "So I have been wondering, are you comfortable in this room or would you like to make changes?"

Looking at me, smiling smugly, Gloria said, "Wow, Christina, you read my mind! I would like to make this space more fun. I want my bookshelf with some of my books in here along that far wall so I can see it from my bed. I'd also like family pictures put on the bookshelf."

"Ok, let's tell Patty what you want and see what she says." I responded.

Heading to the living room I was happy knowing about the positive changes for Gloria and her family. Now, my focus was to help get her room more comfortable. Patty was reading a book when I entered the room. She put it down and smiled at me. I told her what her mom would like to do in her room.

"Oh good, I have asked her several times if she wanted to do that but she didn't seem interested before. I'll call my brothers and ask them to come over this afternoon to help!" She said.

I told Patty I was ready to go home and she said she'd tell her Mom about the plan to call her brothers.

On my drive home that afternoon I felt pride that I was once again able to help Gloria. To know that I had a small part in making her surroundings more pleasurable was very gratifying.

I called her several days later and she was excited to tell me that they had moved the bookshelves for her and made her room very cheerful. She thanked me for all that I had done to help make her last days on earth peaceful and pleasant. I told her that my husband Dave and I would be going on vacation, so I wouldn't be there for a couple of weeks. She was sad but understood. As we said good-bye and hung up the phone an uneasy feeling came over me. I felt sad. Brushing off that feeling with another deep breath, I went on about my day.

Dave and I had a great time at Lake Tahoe, although I kept thinking about Gloria and wondered how she was doing. When we got home I heard the answering machine beeping indicating that we had a voicemail. I rushed to the phone and saw that there were three messages. I pushed the play button and heard the first voicemail. "Chris, it is Mary from Hospice. I know you're on vacation but please call me as soon as you get this voicemail. It's very important." I had a sinking feeling that something had happened to Gloria.

Since I was concerned about what message I was going to hear from Mary, I avoided calling. Instead, I helped empty the car, unloaded my suitcase, and took my time putting things away. Finally, when I couldn't put it off anymore, I called Mary. When she answered, I identified myself and she said, "Hi Chris, thanks for calling. I wanted to let you know that Gloria fell a few days ago and broke her leg and hip. Naturally she's in the hospital so she has been released from Hospice for now."

Relief came over me for a moment, glad that Gloria had not passed away. Then I felt ashamed of myself for being so selfish. Finally sadness came over me that poor Gloria had to tolerate even more physical pain and suffering.

"Thanks Mary, I am sorry that she is having such a bad time physically. I wonder if I should go visit her in the hospital."

"Chris, the tumor on her brain has grown and she is not able to recognize her family anymore. They have her heavily sedated and she isn't awake much. Patty will keep us posted on her condition. Thank you for doing such great work with this family. I'm proud of you!"

Thanking her for her kind words and saying good-bye I placed the phone in the charger base and went to the couch, plunked down and started to cry. I cried happy tears for all the wonderful things that had happened lately to Gloria and her family. I cried sad tears for her continued pain and suffering. I cried tears of grief of my loss, knowing that she would never speak with me again.

Two days later Mary called me to say that Patty had just called her to share that Gloria had passed away a few hours before. She asked Mary to tell me that I had helped their family more than they could express and that they all loved me.

What an honor that was. Making a difference to someone is always very satisfying for me. No matter how much I give to others, doing this work always repays me ten times over. That has always been my experience. From the first assignment on, I have always felt that I receive more than I give.

Tina

Tina was a 43 year old woman who had a cancerous brain tumor. She had fought a good fight for over a year but the cancer spread and although she still had a fighting spirit, her body was giving out. She was married to her high school sweetheart and they had two children, Jason, a senior in high school, and Betsy in eighth grade. Tina was declining rapidly and her husband, Ed, was ready to have a volunteer's help.

My first visit was on a Wednesday morning. I will never forget Ed's smile as he opened the front door. It was obvious that he was grateful to have help. He took me into the family room and pointed to the couch. I sat down and he sat in his chair across the room. I noticed the many vases of flowers that were placed around the room. The mantel was full of cards. It appeared that they were keeping cards from several occasions, birthdays, anniversary, and friendship. Ed shared that Tina liked to come sit in her chair but it was getting harder and harder for her to walk. He said it was fine if I wanted to assist her but I was to remind her that she can no longer stand and walk. She needed to use her cane or hold on to an arm. Tina's short term memory was affected and she needed to be reminded how to do everyday things. He went on to tell me that although Tina had a great sense of humor and had been able to laugh a lot of the time at her situation, there were times when she got very frustrated. During those times, she often yelled and said nasty things. He wanted me to know that so I wouldn't be shocked or insulted.

I thanked Ed for the information and assured him that I would be fine. He got up then and said he would bring Tina out to her chair. While waiting, I looked around the room. The walls were covered with pictures of family. School pictures of their children, wedding pictures, birthday celebrations and pets. I could actually feel the love this family had for each other.

Under the window at the far end of the room was a table that fit under the ledge at the bottom of the window. It was a large table and appeared to be made of heavy oak. Sitting on top of the table was a beautiful collection of egg-shaped stones and glass. The colors were varied and when the sun shined on the table the eggs sparkled. The colors then reflected on the ceiling above the window. I enjoyed looking at the collection.

"Chris, this is Tina, Tina this is Chris." Ed said as he wheeled Tina into the room. I looked at her and smiled and she smiled in return. She was a large woman and she looked a bit uncomfortable in her wheelchair. Her thin hair was pulled back into a ponytail and she wore a wide cloth headband that held the hair back from her face. Ed helped her out of the wheelchair and into the cushioned rocking chair. Once she was settled, he folded the wheelchair up and leaned it against the wall so it would be out of the way. He said, "Tina, I'm going to the store and run errands now. Chris will stay with you until I get back." Turning to me he added, "Chris my cell phone number and the Hospice office phone number are on the fridge if you need to call."

"Thanks Ed, don't worry, we will be fine." I responded. Ed kissed Tina good-bye and left.

Tina and I sat in silence for a few minutes. She appeared to be deep in thought. Slowly smiling at me she said, "Well this is a hell of a mess I have myself in, my fellow Watson." I wasn't sure what to say or do. So I just continued sitting and smiling. She leaned forward in her chair and a serious look came over her face. She said, "Hey, what's your name? Don't you have a sense of humor?"

Chuckling I said, "Yes, Tina, I do have a sense of humor. I just don't know you enough to know that you do too! And my name is Chris."

Tina burst out laughing then and settled back into her chair and began slowly rocking. She did not take her eyes off of me. Finally she said, "Ok, here's the deal. My memory is shot. I often say strange things because this tumor is pressing on my brain. I can be nasty but please don't let me scare or offend you. I'm not a mean person. I promise."

Beaming warmly at her, I said, "It's ok, Tina, I do understand your medical condition and am willing to visit with you. Is there anything you would like me to do during the time I am here?"

"Just visit for now, I think." Tina said.

Ed returned home and was pleased to see that Tina and I were yakking away and laughing together. Tina said, "Hi Honey. Welcome home. We had a great time while you were gone. How long were you away?"

Laughing, Ed put the bags of groceries on the counter and came into the family room. He walked over to Tina, leaned down to give her a kiss. He quietly said, "I was only gone about an hour."

"Wow! Well I had no idea how long you were away but I think I had a bunch of fun. This lady and I laughed a lot." Tina said. She turned to me, "Sorry, I can't remember your name!"

I responded, "It's ok Tina, my name is Chris."

Ed went back into the kitchen and put the groceries away. I gathered my bag and got up to leave. Tina said, "Thank you for the visit. It was fun. I hope you will come back again?"

"I sure will. In fact, I will be coming once a week if that is ok with you?" I asked.

"That sounds perfect!" Tina said.

Ed walked me to the door, "Thanks Chris. Having you here was a huge help to me. It's nice I can run errands and have a normal routine without worrying about Tina, knowing someone is home with her. I look forward to your visit next week."

Turning as I walked out, I said, "You are welcome. I enjoyed my time with Tina very much and look forward to coming back!" Ed watched me until I got into my car. Once I was in, he waved and closed the door.

On my drive home I couldn't help but feel sad for this family. Tina was only 43 years old. Her son was in his senior year of high school. She wanted to be "around" for his senior prom and graduation.

The following week I went to Tina's home as scheduled. As I walked up the sidewalk the front door flew open and there stood Jason. "Hi Chris, I'm glad you came back! Mom is not doing well. She's having more trouble remembering things this week. It's so frustrating for all of us!" Jason exclaimed.

"I'm sorry to hear that Jason." I responded, following him into the house. We went into the family room where Tina was sitting in her rocking chair.

"Who are you and what are you doing here?" Tina said, sounding annoyed.

"Mom, this is Chris from Hospice. I told you she was coming to visit with you while Dad takes me to order my tuxedo." Jason responded, equally annoyed.

"Hi Tina, it's nice to see you again." I said. Tina sat quietly. She didn't pay attention to anyone.

Jason and Ed headed for the garage door, each calling a good-bye.

Tina and I sat in silence. She rocked in her chair and looked around the room. She glanced my way a few times. Finally she said, "I just can't understand why this is happening to me. All I wanted in life was to fall in love, get married and have children. Ed is a wonderful man and I am so grateful he is my husband. We tried for many years to have children. One day our doctor called to say that there was a baby boy available for adoption. We went through a lot of things to adopt Jason, but it finally happened. I remember the day we brought him home. It was one of the happiest days of my life. He was 18 months old and full of love. He laughed a lot. He was so easy to take care of. Ed and I rejoiced in being his parents.

Then our second blessing happened. Betsy was conceived. The day that I found out I was pregnant with her was another happy day. Although I hadn't been feeling real well I was shocked to find out why! I had a good pregnancy, even though I had some medical challenges during that time. Jason and Betsy are very close and I am grateful for that."

Tears streamed down Tina's face. "I am so sad. I wanted to help Jason pick out his tuxedo for the prom. To be in the audience at his graduation, and embarrass him by yelling and screaming his name!"

We sat in silence for a while. When the phone rang, Tina looked over at me and said, "Just let it ring. I don't like to talk on the phone anymore. I may not remember the person anyway and that is very embarrassing."

"Okay, Tina. We'll let the answering machine pick up."

Tina fell asleep in her chair shortly after the phone call. I took my book from my bag and read until Ed and Jason returned home. Jason came into the house calling out to Tina, "Mom! Mom! We found the perfect tux!"

Tina opened her eyes and said, "What tux Jason?"

"For my prom, Mom" He replied. An immediate heaviness came over the room.

"Oh, yes, now I remember." Tina said.

It was tough for me to watch those interactions between Tina and her family. Even though from time to time the family was frustrated, they handled it well. Understanding that Tina's tumor was the cause of her confusion allowed them to work around her memory loss.

Tina's sense of humor endured. She used it to get through some rough times as her illness progressed. During one of my visits she asked me to help her go to the bathroom. Unfortunately, although I did my best to help her get to the toilet in time, we didn't make it. We looked at each other and burst out laughing. I helped her wash up and change her pants. I cleaned up the bathroom while we continued laughing and making jokes of the situation. I helped her back into her bed and she said she was tired. She took a short nap and when she woke up she was surprised that she was wearing different pants. She had no memory of the accident or our fun time together. I felt sad about it but realized that only I remembered what happened. Although I felt sad she didn't remember, I knew that I would always have that fun memory.

My last visit with Tina was amazing. She was bedridden and slept a lot of the time. She had been napping and woke up and asked me my name. I told her and she smiled and said, "Oh yes, Chris. You are an Earth Angel. My grandmother told me that. She said that you have a special gift. You help people who are at the end of their lives. You also help the entire family. That is what you have done for us, Chris. Thank you!" Before I could respond she turned toward the bookshelves across the room from her bed. "Oh! I need to get there!" Tina said, pointing to top shelf.

Following where she was pointing, I looked at the shelf where a cute stuffed teddy bear was placed. "Tina, can I get the bear for you?" I asked.

"No! Chris, I don't need to get the silly teddy bear. I need my Spirit to get to my grandma and she will help me go to the other side. You can't help me, besides that would be cheating. I need to do this by myself. Don't you see her hovering there?" Tina asked.

"No Tina, I don't see her but I'm glad that you do." I responded.

Turning her head towards me, Tina said, "Okay, well she told me to rest some more and that would help me."

"You rest Tina and I will go back to reading my book. I'll be right here though, if you need anything."

Tina smiled at me, blew me a kiss and closed her eyes. She didn't wake again while I was there and never totally regained consciousness. She passed away the following morning, one week before Jason's graduation. I attended her funeral and afterwards I talked to her family. I shared with them what happened during my final visit with her. They were so thankful that she told me about her grandmother coming to get her. They found peace that she was able to tell me what she was experiencing. I was honored to know I was the last person she talked to before she died.

When I first met Tina and her family, I encouraged her to talk with her husband and then told him that she needed to talk. I did that because I was concerned that she would forget. Ed told me after the funeral that he and Tina did talk. He thanked me for being there for all of them. I thanked him for allowing me into their lives during this emotional time.

As I walked to the parking lot Jason called out to me, "Wait Chris! I want to introduce you to my friends. Please don't leave yet!"

Turning to Jason I said, "Hi Jason, sure." He rushed to me then and hugged me tight. I was surprised that a teenage boy would hug me in front of so many other people. He took my hand and guided me to the limousine where his closest friends waited.

He leaned into the car and said, "Guys, this is Chris. The angel I have told you about." He stood back up and released my hand.

His friends said in unison, "Hi Chris, nice to meet you!"

Smiling at them I said, "Hi, nice to meet you too."

Jason hugged me again, "Chris, I am sad that Mom didn't live to see me graduate, but I believe that she will be there in Spirit. She told me she would."

"Yes Jason, I believe she will be watching over you from now on. Good luck in college. Thank you for allowing me to be a part of your family. I'll never forget you."

I think of this family often. I wonder what Jason decided to do for his career; if Ed found another woman to love; and how Tina's daughter is doing. Although this family was in my life for only a short period of time, they will always be remembered.

Colleen

I have been trained in Reflexology. As a result, I have been able to provide either patient support or foot massages for Hospice patients. Usually the patient support assignments are a four hour visit once a week while a foot massage visit is around an hour and a half once a week.

Mary, my volunteer coordinator called me to see if I would consider taking an assignment to do foot massage for a patient to help reduce the daily swelling of her left leg and arm. Immediately I accepted this assignment and was excited because they lived near my home, and I felt good to be serving my community. Often I would be assigned to families in neighboring towns.

Colleen had breast cancer years ago when her daughter was 12 years old. She prayed and asked God to heal her at least until she could raise her daughter to adulthood. Her prayer request was granted and she lived a healthy life until age 60. That is when her cancer returned, this time to her bones. When she had breast cancer she had her left breast removed along with a large number of lymph nodes. This contributed to the swelling in the left side of her body. Her bones were very brittle and sometimes broke with no apparent reason.

Colleen and her husband, Bud, had a close and loving relationship. His job took him out of town sometimes and, as Colleen's illness progressed, they realized the need for help at home. They asked their daughter and her family if they would consider moving in with them to help around the house and with Colleen's care.

Shortly before I was assigned to Colleen, her daughter Vicki, son-in-law Brian, and their three year old daughter, Abby, moved into Colleen and Bud's home.

I was excited to get an appointment to visit Colleen. Vicki picked up the phone on the sixth ring sounding out of breath. I identified myself and told her that the social worker assigned to Colleen had asked me to come do foot massage for her. With excitement in her voice at the suggestion, Vicki asked me to hold while she asked Colleen if she would like that. When she came back to the phone, she said Colleen would love to have me come as soon as I was available. We set a time for my visit and I hung up feeling good and hoping I could help Colleen be more comfortable.

On the day of our appointment I went about my morning routine but my mind was racing and there was an excitement in me that I couldn't identify. The excitement grew as I headed out to Colleen's house later that morning. Once at her home I parked my car, grabbed my travel bag and went to the door.

I rang the door bell but no one answered. I looked at my watch to see if I was early. I rang the bell again and stood there wondering if I had the wrong day. Just as I was turning to head to my car, the door opened slowly and Vicki said, "Christina? Sorry it took me so long to answer the door. Mom fell and I was helping her up."

I was a bit startled and said, "Is she ok? Do I need to come back another time?"

Vicki answered with a sigh, "She's ok, please come in."

Entering the house I followed Vicki down the hall towards Colleen's room. I saw the walls were filled with pictures, the story of this family. Many were candid shots of them laughing and obviously having a good time together. One picture stood out to me, one of Vicki and what I guessed was Colleen, posing next to the elephant exhibit at a zoo. They both looked happy and appeared to have a glow about them. What a contrast when I met her, to how she looked that day. It was obvious she was exhausted. My heart went out to her.

I was greeted with the most delightful smile. Her eyes were beaming! Vicki introduced me to Colleen, left the room, and closed the door. I sat in the chair next to Colleen's bed and put my bag down. She smiled and said, "Welcome Christina, I'm thankful that you are here. What do you have in your bag of tricks?"

As I returned her smile and extended my hand to shake hers I said, "It's nice to meet you. Lotions and towels are in my bag!"

As we shook hands she commented, "Oh, your hand is so warm. It feels wonderful. I can hardly wait for my foot massage!"

Releasing hands, I sat back in the chair and said, "Colleen I'd like to talk a few minutes before I begin the massage. Thank you so much for opening your home to me and allowing me to assist you. It's an honor and I hope to help you feel better by reducing the swelling." She smiled at me and her eyes twinkled as I spoke.

Her immediate response was, "You already have made a difference just by being willing to visit and massage my feet!"

"I have several lotions for you to pick from, one has no fragrance, one has lavender in it and the other cocoa butter. Which would you like me to use?"

Colleen closed her eyes, took a deep breath and held it a moment then released it slowly. She opened her eyes and said, "Lavender please."

I removed a towel and placed it under her feet and pulled the lavender lotion from my bag. Moving the chair so I was directly in front of her right foot I gently took her foot into my hand. She immediately responded saying, "Oh my, that feels wonderful already!" We chatted as I continued the massage. I could sense her relaxing so was quiet as I focused on massaging her. Her eyes were closed and she began to hum quietly. I tried to figure out what she was humming and then it came to me *"How Great Thou Art."* Not only is that one of my favorite hymns of all time, but it brought back wonderful childhood memories for me.

As I finished the massage, the bedroom door flew open and Colleen's granddaughter Abby skipped to Colleen's bedside, her pig tails flopping around her head. "Grandma what are you doing?" She asked. As she asked her question her attention turned to me, and before Colleen could answer, Abby said to me, "Hi. What's your name, and what are you doing to my grandma?"

Colleen and I both laughed and she said, "This is Christina and she is rubbing my hands and feet to make me feel better." Abby smiled at that, and then came around to the end of the bed and climbed up gently, avoiding touching Colleen. She looked at me with her beautiful wide brown eyes and reached her foot out to my hands!

Laughing I said, "Let me wash my hands and then I'll rub your feet. ok?" She nodded her head happily.

As I got up from the chair to wash my hands, Vicki came into the room calling for Abby. She started to scold her for barging into Colleen's room but Colleen stopped her and said it was ok. Vicki was quiet in response to Colleen's command but frustration and concern were on her face.

Vicki followed me out of Colleen's room and stopped me in the hall before I entered the bathroom to wash my hands. She apologized that Abby got away from her and rushed into Colleen's room. She went on to let me know she was fearful that Abby would jump on the bed or somehow accidently bump Colleen and break one of her bones. It hit me then just how fragile Colleen was!

After washing my hands I went back in Colleen's room and found Abby patiently waiting at the end of Colleen's bed with her feet on the towel. Settling back in the chair I asked Abby what lotion she would like me to use on her feet. She grinned and pointed to the bottle of lavender lotion I had just used on Colleen.

When the phone rang Colleen talked to her close friend while I massaged Abby's feet. Abby was ticklish. She wiggled and giggled as I rubbed her feet. I did only five minutes on each foot which was long enough for both of us! As I was finishing Abby's foot massage Colleen ended her phone call. Turning to me with a look of complete relaxation and joy she said, "Thank you so much, Christina, I feel so much better and the swelling has really gone down. Also, thank you for rubbing Abby's feet. That was very kind of you!"

Abby put her flip flops back on and carefully slid off Colleen's bed. She headed out of the room. As she reached the door she turned toward us and said, "Thank you, I have happy feet!" With that she bounced out the door.

As I packed my things into my bag, Colleen laid quietly, her eyes closed and a big smile on her face. I wasn't sure if she was sleeping or just resting but decided to leave and not disturb her to say good-bye. When I got to the door Colleen softly said, "I'm so relaxed and comfortable right now, Christina. It's been a while since I've felt this way. Please come again next week?"

"Sure I'd be glad to come back next week. If you want I'll come twice a week, just let me know. I hope you can rest now."

Colleen spoke again, this time a little louder. "Oh yes, please come twice a week. That would be heavenly! I'm going to take a nap now, please let Vicki know, will you?"

Looking back over my shoulder, I said, "Yes I will, Colleen."

Walking down the hallway I felt full of gratitude for the ability to provide Colleen some pleasure and temporary relief from her illness. I got to the front door and Vicki came toward me from the opposite end of the house. I told her that Colleen was relaxed and comfortable and that she was going to take a nap.

Smiling Vicki said, "Thank you Christina. I hope we see you soon."

"Yes, I'll be back soon. I'll call you tomorrow and set up our next appointment. I told Colleen that I would be glad to come twice a week and she was thrilled. Bye, now."

Once in my car I took a moment to experience the joy I felt from doing this work. I ended up setting a schedule with Colleen to come every Tuesday and Friday at 10:00 AM. I really looked forward to our visits. Colleen and I talked about all kinds of things: her fears for her family after she passed, frustration with her family for not keeping the house as clean and tidy as she did when she was healthy, to her complete acceptance of her disease and her upcoming death. There are stages one goes through in dealing with a diagnosis of a terminal illness. They are; *DABDA - denial, anger, bargaining, depression and then acceptance - Elisabeth Kubler Ross.*

What Colleen struggled with the most was the lack of control over her life. She was so proud of the way she kept her home clean and organized. To her it showed success and that she was a good person. Her family felt she was compulsive about a tidy house and they had to be careful not to disrupt things.

As Colleen worked through her frustration, sadness, fear and anger about her illness, she became less and less concerned about how the house looked. She also shared with me that she finally realized that her family would be fine without her. She hated to admit it, but she knew now her way of doing things wasn't the only correct way. It was just that: her way. All people have their own ways of doing things.

On one visit I was working on Colleen's left foot and we were talking and laughing together when all of a sudden she barely moved her right arm and I heard this horrible snap! It was obvious that a bone in her arm had broken! I looked at her and she smiled and said, "Well there she went! Could you please get Vicki for me?"

I wiped my hands on the towel and jumped up from the chair, and rushed down the hallway. My stomach churned as I looked for Vicki. I found her in the living room brushing Abby's hair. I told her Colleen needed her right away and tried not to let my fear show. She got up immediately and we both hurried back to Colleen's room. She didn't appear to be in pain, but, with Colleen, it was hard to tell because she never complained or showed that she was in pain. Vicki went to the right side of the bed and took one look at Colleen's arm and exclaimed, "Mom! You broke your arm, what happened?"

Colleen replied, 'Nothing dear, I just moved it. Please call Hospice so the nurse can come set it for me."

Sitting in the chair at the foot of the bed I felt my mind racing. I wasn't sure what to do. I sat only a few minutes while Vicki called hospice and Colleen answered their questions. When Vicki hung up the phone, she turned to me, then back to Colleen and said, "Well ladies, Hospice will be here within the half hour to set Mom's arm so it's up to you if you want to continue with the massage or stop." With that, she turned and walked out of the room.

I looked at Colleen waiting for her guidance. She smiled at me and simply said, "Please go back to my massage, it's delightful." I smiled back at her and started working on her left foot to get the swelling down. I was quiet allowing Colleen to relax and focus on the massage. She seemed very comfortable and by the time I finished her massage the hospice nurse arrived. As the nurse came into Colleen's room she greeted me, grinned and said, "Wow, do I get a foot massage after I fix Colleen's arm?" I knew she was kidding but said that I'd be more than happy to do that if she wished.

The next week when I came to visit Colleen I noticed how tired she looked. Her spunk and the twinkle in her eyes were gone. As I sat and prepared for her foot massage, she asked me to wait to set up. She continued to speak, saying she wanted to visit with me first and maybe skip the massage for that day. I was stunned because Colleen loved her massage. I set my bag on the floor and moved the chair to the side of the bed so I was closer to her. Taking a deep breath and closing her eyes she said, "Christina, I'm tired. My body is failing. I am ready to start my journey now but I don't know if my family is okay with that."

We sat in silence for a few minutes. Then Colleen opened her eyes, smiled at me and said, "Ok, please start my massage and we can visit some."

As I put my hand on her foot, reality hit me. Colleen is likely going to die soon. I'm not ready for her to die yet! That thought was such a shock that it sent a chill straight down my spine. Starting the massage I looked at Colleen observing she had been watching me. "A penny for your thoughts, Christina?" She whispered.

Sheepishly I looked at her and said, "It just hit me that you're going to die. Naturally I knew that you would, but today it is very real to me. I'll miss you and our time together. You have taught me so much and I look forward to seeing you twice a week. It will be a huge loss for me once you pass."

Colleen smiled. "I'm honored. I feel like you are a part of my family and I can't thank you enough for all that you have done for us all. You have helped us be calm and live together more comfortably. Now I have another request of you . . . would you please talk to Vicki and Bud and let them know I am really tired of fighting this disease and would like their blessing for me to let go now." With that she closed her eyes and drifted off to sleep.

I cleaned up my massage implements and left her room. Vicki was on the phone in a very spirited conversation and I knew that this would not be the right time to talk with her about Colleen's feelings.

Once home I sat down to write my volunteer progress report notes and burst out crying. This was my first experience of anticipatory grief. Basically I was grieving before Colleen even died! I was surprised by this. I cried for a short time and then collected myself and finished writing my notes. The more I thought about my conversation with Colleen, the more I realized I should talk to the volunteer coordinator so that we could get the social worker involved. Once I identified what to do, I was relieved. I hadn't realized my stress was because I was unsure of how to handle a conversation about Colleen wanting to let go with family members. That isn't the volunteer's role. The proper procedure is to call and report what the patient said, document her statements in the volunteer notes and let Hospice take it over from there.

I visited Colleen twice more and by the second visit she asked me just to sit with her rather than do massage work. It was amazing how I could feel the difference in her energy level. She was obviously very tired and yet she wanted me there with her. I sat in the chair at the foot of the bed, where I usually sit. She asked me to move the chair closer to the head of her bed so that we could visit easily. She didn't have the energy to talk louder than a whisper.

Once settled in the chair I asked her what she wanted me to do. She opened her eyes, smiled, and said, "I'd like you to hold my hand. Having you here helps keep me peaceful inside."

That was a wonderful compliment that filled my heart with love, compassion and sadness all at once. I would truly miss my visits with Colleen. It was obvious that her time was coming soon. We sat for about a half hour, in total silence. During that time I thought about previous visits with her and how much fun we had together. It felt good to know my massage gave her physical relief from extreme swelling and discomfort. We so enjoyed each other that the time together was a benefit for both of us.

Colleen stirred, opened her eyes which were full of tears. "Christina, you are doing God's work. I can't thank you enough for all you have done for me. I am ready to die soon so this will be our last visit together. Please know I will be eternally grateful to you. I am ready to sleep now so you can go."

With tears in my eyes and a lump in my throat that felt like I had swallowed a golf ball, I said, "Colleen, thank you so much for allowing me into your life at such a personal time. I'm thankful I was able to assist you and please know it was truly an honor. I will never, ever forget you, my friend." Bending over Colleen's bed I gently kissed her forehead, told her I loved her, and prepared to leave the room. Just as I got to the door I turned back to take one last look at Colleen, unable to hold back my tears.

She smiled at me and with the most angelic voice she said, "I love you too, my earth angel."

My drive home that day was bittersweet. I knew this was the last time I made the drive to and from Colleen's home and spending quality time with a wonderful woman. Three days later I receive the expected phone call from Mary at Hospice sharing that Colleen had passed away peacefully in her sleep the night before. I asked that she call me when they had the funeral information since I don't usually attend the funeral of patients, this was one patient whose funeral I needed to attend.

The church was packed. There must have been 400 people there. I felt honored to be among them. I came with her hospice case manager who had been very close to Colleen. We found a place to sit. As we waited for the service to start I looked at the program they gave us when we entered the sanctuary. I was thrilled to see a couple of Colleens' profound poems she had written during her dying experience. As I read the poems I recalled some of my visits with her. At one, she read a few of her poems out loud to me. Again my tears came. I stopped reading and dabbed my eyes. The funeral was a wonderful tribute to

Colleen's life. People in the congregation shared funny and heartwarming stories about their experiences with Colleen.

I left her funeral feeling a sense of closure and inner peace, that I had attended and shown my last respect.

I learned so much about life from Colleen. She shared the value of surrounding yourself with people who believe in you so when you are down you know you have someone who will be there for you. My visits with Colleen always ended with her sharing wisdom that gave me a lot to ponder. I think of Colleen often and have a good feeling inside knowing she is still supporting me!

Misty

Each assignment is special and unique and teaches me different pieces of wisdom. One common thing that happens near the end of life is that people say they see angels and/or loved ones that have passed over. They often talk with those they see. My experience with Misty took that to another level, which I found interesting and made me very curious.

They called me on a Thursday to see if I would be willing to take an assignment for Friday morning for four hours. Misty was in the end stages of cirrhosis of the liver. I was shocked to hear that she was only 33 years old. She was living with her parents, who had custody of Misty's two daughters. Misty's mother, Nancy, had just been diagnosed with breast cancer and was starting treatment the next day. Her father needed to take her mother to the hospital for treatment so they needed someone to sit with Misty during that time. Her best friend, Suzie, was not available. The Hospice social worker was able to convince the family to allow a volunteer to come. I accepted the assignment immediately.

Driving to Misty's home the next morning I was very curious what my time would be like during this visit. I couldn't help but wonder what her life had been like to have such a horrible disease so young. After parking the car, I grabbed my bag and headed to the front door.

Almost as soon as I rang the doorbell Edgar, Misty's father, opened the door. He greeted me with a big smile, extended his hand for a shake and introduced himself. He thanked me for coming on such short notice.

"It's not a problem. I enjoy helping others when I can." I responded.

Edgar asked me to follow him and we went into the family room where he offered me a seat on the couch. He sat in a chair across from me and said, "Misty is in the front bedroom sleeping. She sleeps for many hours at a time so don't worry if she doesn't wake up while you are here. I just gave her medication and she can sleep four or five hours after she takes it. She does know that you will be here while I take Nancy to the hospital so if she wakes up she won't be frightened." Nodding, I smiled at him. He went on to say, "Our phone rings a lot these days so please don't answer it. Let the answering machine pick up. OK?"

"Sure, that's not a problem. Are there any other specific instructions you have for me?" I asked.

"Well, Misty's friend Suzie may come over. She is working but she is taking as much time off as possible to spend with Misty." Edgar said, sadness in his voice. "She is taking this very hard. They have been best friends since kindergarten. Suzie has been through so much with all of Misty's ups and downs. Misty has made some very bad decisions in her life and Suzie has always been there without judgments. That is the real meaning of a true friend. She has been there when we couldn't be. It has been painful and there are still a lot of resentments and unresolved issues among Misty, my wife, and me. It's sad but we are doing the best we can for Misty and for our granddaughters. They are the innocent ones in this entire mess. So, if Suzie comes while you are here, will you please give her the opportunity to talk to you?"

Misty's Mom, Nancy came into the room then and Edgar introduced us. She thanked me for coming. As she led me on a tour of their home, she showed me the phone number list in the kitchen should I need to call them on the cell phone, or need to call Hospice. She shared her concern that Misty was rapidly declining. Nancy and Edgar left for the hospital with a final "Thank you".

I gathered my bag and went down the hall to Misty's bedroom. There I saw that she lay on her side facing the wall. I couldn't see her face. She was breathing heavy and I was a bit startled when she started moaning. I sat in the chair next to her bed, listening and watching. Silence filled the room for about five minutes. All of a sudden, I had the strongest desire to write a letter to Misty. This had never happened to me before, but I got my notebook and pen and began to write. Holding tightly to the pen, my fingers felt as if someone else were guiding them. *"I sit here next to you. It is so very quiet. I sense that your energy is depleting. I listen to your inconsistent breathing; occasional moans and I wonder if you are dreaming. What are you dreaming about? What can I do for you today Misty? Other than pray for you, which I have already done. I have asked God to give you peace as you leave this world. I find it easier now to just "be." I've been here before, and know that this is sometimes all that is needed. Although this is familiar to me . . . it is interesting how loud the quiet can be!*

The phone rings over and over, but I was told to let the answering machine pick up. It's odd for me to hear the phone ring and not get up and answer it. My job for today is to sit next to you and just be here for you. As I watch you sleeping, I only see your face from the side as it is tilted toward the wall. Your skin is very yellow, a sign of your failing liver. I notice your uneven breathing and moaning. Are you experiencing physical discomfort or feeling alone? I reach over to gently touch you...and you relax...your moaning ceases and your breathing seems more regular. I thank you, God, for allowing me the privilege of being with Misty today. It is an honor to be with her at this time in her life.

Misty, will you wake while I am here? Will you turn your face this way so that I can see it? Will this be the only time that I come to sit with you? They say that your disease will most likely take you from this world in a couple of weeks. Is that so? Your Mom told me you have seen angels, one of them being your Grandmother. Has God sent her to let you know your time is near but to not fear? Is she here to take you by the hand and lead you into eternity? So many questions come to my mind, yet I will never ask you them. I will return to sit with you on Tuesday morning if you are still in this world. I am grateful to you and your family for allowing me into your lives at such a personal and intimate time. They are very special people. Hopefully, I have been of help to your family today. Blessings sweet lady, may your passing be peaceful."

Misty didn't waken or turn her head during that visit. When her parents returned I told Misty goodbye and that I would return the following Tuesday to sit with her. I left her room feeling very connected to her, although we had no personal interaction.

The following Tuesday I returned to sit with Misty. Nancy took me into the bedroom, this time Misty was awake, and Nancy introduced us. I smiled at Misty and she just looked at me. I noted a blank look on her face, yellow from her illness. The area around her eyes was so dark she appeared to have black eyes. Nancy asked Misty if she would like to sit in the family room to visit with me while she and Edgar went out. Misty replied angrily, "No! Just leave me alone Mother. Stop talking. Get out of my room, all of you!"

I turned and immediately left the room. Nancy said something further to Misty that I couldn't hear and then she came out. We walked into the family room and sat down. Nancy was holding back tears but finally they streamed down her face. Her eyes were the saddest I have seen. "Misty is so angry." She said. "She is actually angry with herself but lashes out at all of us. I know logically this is displaced anger, but it breaks my heart when she yells at us."

After a few seconds of silence, I reached over and took Nancy's hand in mine. "I am sorry for all of the pain you and your entire family are experiencing. I wish I could make it better. Knowing I can't, I want you to know I'm here for all of you. The entire Hospice team is available. Please don't hesitate to call on any of us."

Nancy squeezed my hand and said, "Thank you, that really does help. Edgar and I will be back in a few hours."

As they left the house, I went back to Misty's room to see if she wanted anything. As I approached, I heard her talking on the phone. I stopped at the doorway and she looked up to me and offered a slight smile. She put her finger up as if to say "wait a minute." I stood quietly as I waited for her to end the phone call. Closing her cell phone, she said, "Sorry about earlier. My parents are really getting on my nerves. I wasn't upset with you. Please sit down."

I sat down in the same chair where I spent most of my first visit with her. "Thanks Misty. It's nice to meet you. Is there anything in particular I can do for you while I'm here?"

"Can you save my life and make this nightmare go away?" Misty responded.

"No, unfortunately I can't do that. I'm here because I want to help when possible."

Misty didn't say anything. We sat in silence for a short time, and then she let out a huge sigh and said, "Ok, once again I'm sorry. I don't mean to be so snotty to you. None of this is your fault. I would like to go into the family room now. Will you get my walker for me, please?"

"Sure."

I got up from the chair and went to get her walker. I put it next to her and helped her stand. Once she had her balance, she started towards the family room. The phone rang. "Just let it ring. I don't want to talk to anyone." She said, adding, "It's probably for Mom anyway."

We went into the family room. After she was settled in the recliner in the corner of the room she said, "Now, I want to know something about you. Why do you do this work, especially for free?"

"I enjoy helping others. I hope I make a difference when I come to people's homes during a time like this." I said cheerfully.

Misty didn't respond. She stared out the glass patio doors looking toward the small garden. "That is where I like to sit. I love that little garden. It is such a peaceful place. Before I got sick I never sat out there. I didn't have a second thought about it at all. I was so focused on other things I would never take the time to sit down and be quiet and just enjoy nature. You know something, Chris, I like this family room and I like being able to see out the patio doors. I would love to put my bed out here. I hate being stuck in the bedroom at the back of the house. Even though the other bedrooms are back there, during the day I'm alone. It would be much nicer to be here in the family room."

"Well Misty, maybe you can talk with your parents to arrange that."

"You don't know them. They aren't likely to agree, just to keep me miserable. Pay back from all that I have put them through over the years. I bet that is what they will say." Frustration was in her voice.

We sat in silence for a while and before long Misty fell asleep in the chair. I had a book with me, so I took it out of my bag and began to read. About a half hour later Nancy and Edgar came home. They were surprised to see Misty asleep in the chair in the family room. I put my book back into my bag and got up, following Nancy into the kitchen.

"Nancy, I had a heart-to-heart talk with Misty while you were gone and she expressed a desire. I suggested she mention it to you and Edgar but she didn't think you would be open to it. Would you like me to tell you?" I asked.

"Hmmm. Well, actually I will approach her and tell her what you said and ask her to tell me. I hope you don't mind, but I'd rather talk with her directly. That has been a huge part of our troubles with Misty, the lack of communication." Nancy replied.

"I don't mind at all. That's great! I'll head on home now and see you next week."

"Yes, next week." Nancy replied happily and walked me to the front door.

Arriving at Misty's home the following week I noticed several cars parked in the driveway, which seemed unusual. I parked on the street and went to the front door. I rang the doorbell several times before Marla, Misty's oldest daughter, answered the door. "Oh, hi Chris!" She said. "Come in. Aunt Rose and Uncle George are here. Suzie is here too."

I put my purse and bag on the entry hall table. Nancy came out to greet me and led me into the family room to meet the relatives. Much to my surprise I saw Misty in a hospital bed. I was pleased she could see the patio doors, and the garden beyond. I smiled and said to Nancy, "I see you agreed with Misty's request!"

Nancy responded, "Yes, I have no idea why she would think that we wouldn't want her in this room but it has worked out well. She seems much more comfortable in here than being in her room." Nancy introduced me to family members. We shook hands and exchanged pleasantries. I noticed dramatic changes in Misty from last week when I visited. Her face was a darker shade of yellow. Her eyes were a bit sunken and she looked very thin and frail.

"Hi Chris, how are you?" Suzie asked. I turned and saw her sitting on the couch. Although she smiled at me, I could see the pain and sadness she was feeling. How hard it must be for her to watch her best friend slowly passing at such a young age. Nancy had told me about Suzie's friendship with Misty. Suzie had sat with her and put up with all the times when Misty was angry and lashing out. Suzie asked, "Can we go out in the living room to talk?"

"Of course."

We went into the living room, and I took a seat on the couch next to Suzie. "How are you doing?" I asked.

Suzie looked down at her lap for a moment before answering. "This is tough, no doubt about it. But, I'm grateful that my boss is understanding and gives me time off so that I can come and be with Misty." After another moment of silence, she said, "Chris, do you see how much Misty has gone downhill?"

"Yes. It may be getting close to the end now. Have you told her everything you need too? Have you given her your permission to let go?"

Suzie sighed, "Not in those words. I have tried to tell her that I will help with the girls and look out for her parents. It didn't occur to me to come right out and say it's ok to die."

"If you are truly supportive of her letting go, I encourage you to tell her." I said. "Give her the opportunity to talk to you about her feelings on dying. If she doesn't want to talk about it that is ok."

We sat in silence for a few minutes while Suzie thought about what I said. Then she rose to her feet. "Thank you Chris. I am going to go talk with her. Do you mind giving us a few minutes alone?"

"Not at all, I'll stay out here in the living room and read. Please come get me when you are done." I picked up my book as she left the room.

Edgar came in and told me the family had left and he and Nancy were heading out too. He also said that Suzie was in with Misty having a private conversation. I told him that everything would be fine here. He thanked me and left.

After 30 minutes Suzie came into the living room and sat in the chair across from me. It was a cozy bay window area with two chairs and a small antique desk between the chairs. On top of the desk was a lamp made of stained glass. I put my book down on my lap and looked over at Suzie. Her eyes and nose showed she had been crying. Sadness in her voice, she said, "Chris that was an amazing conversation. She was so relieved to talk about what is happening to her. She told me she is ready to die because she knows she can't get better. She is also frightened. We talked about her concerns that she doesn't know what will happen when she dies. She isn't afraid of pain because the Hospice Nurse provided medication and she has not been in pain. She is fearful she will have repercussions from choices she made in her life."

Leaning toward me she continued, "When she was eight years old she started drinking. She was very unhappy as a young child, and made friends with older kids in our neighborhood. I told her over and over she was going to get into trouble if she hung around with them. She wouldn't listen to me. We remained best friends even though she spent time with others.

By the age of ten she experimented with marijuana, which led to many parties she shouldn't have attended. When Misty was 15 she was raped by one of the young men she drank and did drugs with. All of this led to her being angry and a continuing cycle of bad decisions.

She thanked me for talking so openly with her and giving her my permission to let go. She said she is going to take a nap but you can go sit in the family room whenever you want. I need to go back to work now. Thank you for your suggestion. I feel better after talking with Misty. I am very sad and know she won't be here for very long. I will miss her but I am comforted knowing that she will soon be free of this body that isn't working any longer. I said everything I wanted to say to her. Thanks again."

Suzie and I stood and walked to the front door. As she opened it she reached out and gave me a one arm hug, "What wonderful work you do, Chris. I admire you. It takes a very special person to work with terminally ill people. Bless you."

"Thanks for your kind words, Suzie." I said smiling and watched Suzie walk out to her car.

I went back into the family room. Misty was asleep. I walked to the couch, sat down and opened my book. After about an hour, the phone rang. It startled me and instinctively I got up and walked toward the kitchen to answer it. Just before I reached the phone I remembered that the family wanted me to let all calls go to the answering machine. I turned and went back to the couch. I sat back down and Misty said, "Chris, are you there?" I saw that her eyes were open but she was staring at the patio doors.

At her bedside I said, "Yes Misty, I'm here. Did you need something?"

Not moving her eyes from the patio door she said, "Look over there, do you see?"

I looked at the doors and answered, "No Misty, I don't see anything other than the doors and the garden outside."

"Wow, you don't see her standing by the doors?" Misty said loudly.

"No, I don't, who is it? Do you know her?" I asked.

With excitement in her voice now Misty said, "It's me! Shit, it's me! Can't you see me over there?"

Astonished, I said, "No! I can't see you but I believe that you can see yourself."

Leaning back in the chair I took a deep breath and released it slowly. We sat in silence for a minute or so and then Misty started laughing. Her laughter got louder and then she started singing "Halleluiah! Halleluiah! I'm going to live on!"

I listened until she became quiet. Then she turned to me with a smile. One big tear ran down her right cheek. "Man, Chris that was a trip. Now I get it. I am going to die and leave this physical body. In fact I think that will happen soon. I'm ready now because I'm not scared anymore. I know my Spirit will live on in the next dimension of life. It's time to shed this body that no longer works, mostly because of what I did to it. But I don't feel guilty anymore. There is no need. I am sorry but no longer feel guilty. Please tell my parents. Promise you will tell my parents?" She asked.

"Okay Misty, I will tell your parents what happened and what we talked about if you are sure you want me to."

Smiling, Misty reached out to me and grabbed my hand in hers. "Yes, please tell them everything. I am so tired now and I want to take another nap. You can go back to the couch if you want, or you can sit here with me until I go to sleep."

"I'll sit with you until you go to sleep." I answered. Still holding my hand Misty let another tear slip down her cheek. She closed her eyes. She was asleep within a few minutes and I continued to hold her hand for a short time. I silently listened to her steady breathing. This time she did not moan. She looked peaceful. Gently releasing her hand I got up from the chair and went back to the couch. Picking up my book I settled in to read until Misty's parents returned home.

Nancy and Edgar entered the family room. Misty was sleeping and didn't wake when they arrived. I put my book into my bag and got up from the couch. Nancy took the chair beside Misty. Edgar and I walked out to the living room. I told Edgar about my time here with Misty. As I talked, he began to cry softly but he smiled at the same time. He was quiet for a few minutes after I shared with him.

Clearing his throat he said, "That is amazing. I can't thank you enough for all you have done for us, including Suzie. I am so glad that Misty is no longer afraid to let go. I'm also going to tell her it's ok to let go. I hope that will help her. I don't know if Nancy can say that yet. I will tell Nancy everything you shared with me and that may help her prepare as well."

Edgar and I went back to the family room. I went to Misty's bed, Nancy still sat in the chair next to the hospital bed, but they were not talking. Misty was drifting in and out of sleep. Taking her hand in mine I leaned over and whispered in her ear, "Thank you Misty for sharing your life with me. I will never forget you. I wish you a peaceful passing. You have a special place in my heart." I kissed her on the forehead and released her hand.

She opened her eyes, winked at me, and said, "Bye now."

Edgar walked me to the front door and thanked me again. I gave him a hug and went to my car, noting that he remained at the door. He waved and I pulled away.

That was the last time I saw Misty and her family. She died in her sleep the following morning. I was happy to know I had helped this family talk openly and clear away some of their misunderstandings. Misty was able to have a peaceful end to a very stressful and dramatic life.

Brenda

Some assignments are a one-time only. Often they are requests made on the spur of the moment. So when the volunteer coordinator called to ask if I would consider doing a foot massage the following day I wasn't sure I could because I had another appointment in the afternoon. She went on to explain that the patient, Brenda, was in the end stages of emphysema and her feet were very swollen and uncomfortable. Brenda lived close to my home, so I said I would be able to do it in the morning if that worked for the patient.

Shortly after my conversation with the volunteer coordinator, I called Brenda. She answered the phone in the middle of a coughing fit and asked me to hold a moment. When she came back to the phone I introduced myself and offered to visit her in the morning. She said she would love to have me come and thanked me. She sounded tired and struggled to talk so I told her I'd be there at 10 the following morning and we hung up.

As I arrived at Brenda's home, I smelled cigarette smoke. A sign on her front door said, "Caution Oxygen in Use." I was a bit concerned, noticing that the smoke odor was coming from Brenda's home! Since this was a duplex, I was concerned about the neighbors' safety. I knocked on the door and heard Brenda yell, "Come in, Chris."

Opening the door cautiously I entered the living room. Brenda lay on her hospital bed, wearing her oxygen, and smoking a cigarette! I couldn't believe my eyes. I dropped my bag on the floor and asked her to put out her cigarette before I started her foot massage.

Immediately she was angry and yelled at me. "No! This is my home and I'll smoke if I want." She glared at me.

I calmly picked up my bag. "Yes Brenda, it is your right to smoke in your home but it is not safe to smoke while wearing an oxygen mask and I'm not comfortable being in your home with that danger. Feel free to call the Hospice office if you want to reschedule but I won't be able to stay if you are smoking." I started to walk to the door.

"Wait, Chris! Please come back. I'll put my cigarette out." Brenda called. She put the cigarette out in the bulging ashtray at her bedside.

I returned to her bed and sat down to prepare for her foot massage. I remained quiet as I set up and she watched my every move. When I was ready I said, "Ok Brenda, are you ready for me to begin?"

She smiled sheepishly, "Yes, thank you for staying. I am sorry I lashed out at you."

Throughout the foot massage Brenda and I chatted. She told me that she was very angry to be "in this situation," and that she realized she was not going to make it out of this episode. She went on to tell me she had not been well for years, all because of the stupid choice she made as a teenager. She went to a party with some girlfriends in ninth grade. The group had cigarettes and as soon as they sat down they lit up. She was the only one that didn't smoke but by the end of the party they had convinced her to try it. Although she didn't really enjoy it, she smoked several cigarettes during the party to be cool and fit in. Soon it became a habit and now, 30 years later she was dying from complications of smoking.

I listened to her story as I massaged her feet and when she stopped talking, I felt I could ask her a few questions. "Brenda, what good does it do to be so angry now, and exactly who are you angry with?"

After a few moments of silence Brenda answered, "Well, I'm angry because I'm dying at a young age. I don't want to die, I want to live. I'm angry with those girls who made me smoke."

I remained quiet, allowing Brenda more time to think about her situation. Finally she said, "I guess I'm most angry with myself. I was weak and gave in to peer pressure and allowed myself to become addicted to something that I knew wasn't good for my health. I just didn't think I would develop cancer. I always believed that cancer attacks other people, not me." She closed her eyes.

Brenda and I remained silent for the rest of her foot massage. When I finished, I asked to use her bathroom to wash my hands. "Of course you can. It's down the hall, the first door on the right. Thank you for that massage. It felt wonderful."

Entering the bathroom I washed my hands and noticed the beautiful Native American decorations on the wall. Returning to the living room I said, "Brenda, I noticed the beautiful dream catchers in your bathroom, I really like them."

"Oh, thank you." Brenda beamed at me. "I'm Native American and proud of my heritage. I made some of those dream catchers myself."

"Wow, very nice!" I exclaimed. I stayed and visited with Brenda who shared pictures of her life, her crafts, and her stories. She said her feet felt so much better after the massage and that she enjoyed our visit. She apologized again for being snotty and stubborn when I first arrived.

Although this was only a one-time visit, I felt good knowing that I had made a difference in her life. On my drive home that day, I was happy knowing that I had weathered this patient's anger and helped her come to a place of enjoying the moment and making the best of her life for however long it would be. I was grateful I had the courage to refuse treatment when oxygen and fire were so close together. It helped me know that setting boundaries as well as consoling patients is an important part of my work.

≈ ≪

Bill and Vern

Bill was in the end stages of emphysema after many years of discomfort. His friend Vern moved in to assist in caring for him. As Bill's health declined he and Vern became more and more reclusive. By the time I was called to sit with Bill so Vern could go to his own doctor appointment, he was emotionally and physically exhausted.

As I parked my car I noticed that even though it was a beautiful sunny day the two men kept the curtains closed. Vern came out just as I was getting out of my car. "Oh, are you my volunteer?" He asked.

"Yes I am." I held out my hand. He gave me a firm handshake. He wore a slight smile but I could see pain and sadness in his eyes.

"Thanks so much for coming. I really need a break." He said. "I'll explain things to you once we are inside."

As I followed him up the wheelchair ramp to the front door I wondered what he would say. Once inside the home he pointed to an overstuffed recliner indicating that he wanted me to sit down.

Bill and Vern had a wonderful dog named Sassie. She was an eleven-year-old German Shepard and she didn't like most people. Vern told me about Sassie and said that he had locked her in his bedroom because he was concerned she may try to bite me. I told him that I liked dogs but he felt it best to leave her in his room.

As I sank into the comfy and very used chair I said, "Are there specific things you would like me to do while I'm here?"

After a few seconds he said, "Yes, I want to know that while I am gone you will give full attention to Bill and make him feel special."

"Sure! Is there anything you can suggest that will help me make him feel special?"

Again Vern took his time answering me. "Well, Bill is a very large man and usually people are shocked when they see him. Often they show disgust at his size. If you would give him that beautiful smile like you gave me, he will absolutely feel special. I did."

That took me somewhat aback, but I assured him that I would smile at Bill and asked that he take me into Bill's room and introduce us. Vern said that Bill wanted to come to the living room to meet me and he would get him right away.

As I waited for Vern to bring Bill, I looked around the living room. It was dark because of the closed curtains. The next thing I noticed was that the room was starkly furnished. No decorations. The pieces were functional but not warm and inviting.

Vern pushed Bill in his wheelchair into the living room. I offered my broadest smile as I looked at Bill. His first response was a look of surprise but he smiled back at me. I immediately felt his warmth! Vern pushed Bill near me so we were facing each other, a comfortable distance apart. Vern then said, "Chris I'm glad to introduce you to my dear friend, Bill."

I extended my hand saying, "Hi Bill, it's an honor to meet you."

Bill's smile widened as we shook hands. "Oh Chris, the honor is mine! Thanks for coming to visit today!"

Vern said, "I'm going to my doctor appointment. I have my cell phone with me, should you need anything. Enjoy your visit." With that, he picked up his backpack and headed for the front door.

Bill and I sat quietly for a few minutes after Vern left. It was a comfortable silence. I wanted to wait until Bill spoke. He adjusted himself in his wheelchair. "This is so nice, Chris. Vern and I have been alone in this home for so long and haven't had much contact from others until I started with Hospice. Now we have a nurse, a CNA, a social worker and a chaplain coming in. I'm so grateful to have this service and am pleased you can visit. I don't like being so dependent on Vern. He's tired and a bit resentful. When I ask him how he's doing he answers 'Fine.' I know that isn't really true. I see the hurt and sadness in his eyes, and the physical changes in him. I know he is worn out and needs time for himself."

"Well now that I can visit you, Vern will have the opportunity to go out and do whatever he wants. It's up to him to take care of himself and allow the Hospice team to assist you in any way we can. I do want to know how you are feeling about what is happening to you now. If there is anything in particular I can do for you, please let me know." I relaxed leaning back into the soft chair.

"Make yourself at home for starters." Bill said with a smile. "I know I don't have much time left. My heart can give out at any moment. I am not afraid to die. I am, however, fearful of what will happen to Vern once I pass. He has focused on me and my needs and shut everyone else out of his life. He is alone except for me. He has even excluded family and friends from his life, which saddens me. People have been vicious to us, making all kinds of assumptions and accusations that we are a gay couple. Many of his family and friends believe that life style is a sin and that God will not accept gay people.

I silently allowed Bill to process what he told me, to see if he would continue talking or if he expected me to respond. Bill bowed his head slightly, looking at his feet. He appeared comfortable and deep in thought. Looking up, he smiled and resumed speaking. "Chris, thank you for being here. For giving me this time to talk to you, and to talk out loud to myself. I have had these thoughts swirling around in my head for days now. It feels good to say them out loud. I also want to thank you for not saying anything. The quiet time let me judge how much I could tell you and how you might respond. Your silence told me you are safe. I can say what I feel and you are open and willing to just listen. Now, I do have some questions for you. Is that ok?"

"Sure Bill. What would you like to know?"

"I want to know why you do this work, especially on a volunteer basis." Bill asked.

"Bill, I do this work because I was born to serve. I feel God created us with individual abilities and talents and this is one of mine. As for volunteering my time, I am fortunate my husband works and we live comfortably on his salary. The reward I get from doing this work is priceless. I always feel I have received more than I give with every assignment. It makes me feel good when I do something for others. Making a difference fills my spirit!"

"Wow, Chris. That is beautiful." Bill responded softly. "What a wonderful way to live your life. You have truly figured out how you can do what you love and it works for you. That is rare."

Just then we heard a loud "Woof!" "Have you met Sassie yet?" Bill asked.

"No, Vern was concerned that she might try to bite me so he said he would leave her in his room."

"Are you afraid of dogs?" Bill asked.

"Not at all, I love dogs."

Bill straightened in his chair, released the brakes and said, "I'll get her. Hopefully she will behave." He pushed himself to Vern's room and opened the door. Sassie came running out, barking and carrying on. I sat still, didn't move, or speak. Bill followed Sassie into the living room and said, "Sassie! Quiet. It's ok." He then patted his leg and Sassie ran to his side and put her head in his lap. She calmed down as he lovingly stroked her.

I decided to talk to Sassie and see what her response would be. "Hi Sassie" I said. She looked at me, then at Bill and then slowly walked over to me. I held out my hand and she sniffed it. I gently patted her head. She sat still, seeming to enjoy it. Then suddenly, she jumped into my lap! She was a large dog and I found myself crushed into the back of the chair. Bill yelled at Sassie to "get down". She did jump down but didn't leave the side of the chair where I sat. She leaned against my leg. I was surprised because Vern had been so concerned that she would bite me. Sassie kept nudging me with her nose. Finally I said to Bill. "I think she wants to sit close to me. Shall I sit on the floor, or is she allowed on the furniture?"

A large smile lit Bill's face, "Oh sure! She's allowed on the couch that has the throw cover on it."

Getting up from the chair I walked to the couch. As I sat down, Sassie jumped up with me. She kissed my neck, face and then lay down right next to me, placing her paw in my lap. Bill burst out laughing and I joined in. Realizing that she was the center of attention, Sassie made funny noises, and rolled around on the couch. It was a lot of fun.

Just then, Vern came in the front door and stopped dead in his tracks. First a look of shock, then a huge smile lit his face as he said, "Well now, I never expected to see Sassie out, let alone sitting with you, Chris!" Chuckling, he put his backpack down and sat at the opposite end of the couch. Sassie turned to him and gave him kisses while her tale wagged back and forth in my face!

Bill was ready to go back to bed. Since Vern was home, I decided it was a good time for me to leave. I hugged Bill good-bye and Vern walked me to my car. Standing next to me, he said, "Thanks so much for coming. I really needed this time to get some things done for myself. How do you feel about coming back next week?"

"I would love to come back next week. Shall we make Thursdays my regular day to visit?"

Once again Vern looked surprised. "Wow, yes it will be great if I can count on you to come each week. Then I will be able to make plans ahead of time. This is wonderful." Vern reached out and grabbed me. I hugged him back and noticed a tear trickling down his cheek. He held my door open for me as I got in and shut it once I was in. I started the car and rolled the window down. Vern still stood next to the car, "Again, thank you Chris. You have no idea what an angel you are for us! I look forward to seeing you next week!"

"I look forward to returning. Have a good week and I'll call to check in on Wednesday."

I called the next Wednesday to double-check. When Vern answered the phone, I knew something was wrong. I identified myself and immediately he began crying. "What's wrong Vern?"

"Bill has taken a turn for the worse, Chris. I don't think he's going to rebound this time. He's sleeping most of the time now. He had a few really good days after your visit. We had some great heart-to-heart talks. Then, just before bed, he told me that it was time for him to let go. He thanked me for all I had done for him and apologized for creating a situation that made others think we are a gay couple. We aren't. We are friends who love and respect each other and don't have others we can depend on."

"Vern, do you want me to come tomorrow? Even if you want to be there too, is there anything that I can do for you?"

Sighing heavily, Vern said, "No Chris. You have been such a huge help already. I just want to stay by Bill's side until he passes. I want you to know, because of your visit with Bill he was able to talk with me openly and share his concerns and his desires. He said you were such a help to him just by listening. We are both forever grateful to you for helping us so much in one visit. Even Sassie loves you!"

I thanked him for his kind words and asked him to tell Bill I thanked him too. I also asked Vern to tell Bill goodbye for me and give him a hug. He cried softly and that made me start to cry. He said, "Again, thanks for all you do. You are an Earth

Angel for many. I'm thankful you were for us. I'm going to go back to Bill now. Love you, my new friend."

With a huge lump in my throat, I said, "Love you too. Please take care of yourself and thank you for opening your home to me."

Hanging up the phone I felt sad knowing that Bill was making his transition but also fulfilled, knowing that in one visit I had made a difference in their lives.

Bill peacefully passed the following Saturday afternoon with Vern sitting at his side. What a blessing it is for people to have the Hospice services available so that they can die in their homes, with family and loved ones surrounding them.

Jack and Sally

Jack was at the end of his life and totally bedridden. He slept most of the time. After taking care of Jack non-stop for weeks, Sally finally asked for a volunteer to come sit with him so that she could get her hair done. I accepted this one-time assignment and had no idea what I was about to experience.

Sally was thrilled when I arrived. She rushed outside and greeted me at the car. As I got out and closed the door, she extended her hand and said, "Chris, I'm Sally. I'm so glad to meet you."

"It's nice to meet you too, Sally." I followed her into the house. Jack was asleep in the living room on a hospital bed. She pointed to a chair across the room where I sat down. "Jack, honey, this is Chris. She is going to stay here with you while I go get my permanent. I'll be back in a couple of hours. I love you."

Jack was sound asleep and didn't respond. Sally kept talking. She didn't seem concerned that Jack was not listening. She turned to me and started talking about Jack then, as if he wasn't there. That seemed very strange to me, and I felt uncomfortable.

"Chris. I just don't know what to do. Jack is the love of my life and we have been married for 49 years and I have already planned our 50th anniversary party. Now I'm not sure we will have that party. Jack may not live that long. That breaks my heart. In fact, when he dies I want to go with him." She paused, then looking directly into my eyes, she said, "I am not willing to live alone. Jack is my life and I know I won't want to be here without him."

Drawing a deep breath I said, "Sally, I must tell you this: If you are saying what I think you are, you must stop. First of all, if you are considering suicide, then I will have to report that to Hospice. Second, knowing how hard it will be for you and your daughter when Jack dies, think about how hard it would be for your daughter to have both of you die around the same time. Suicide is a permanent solution to a temporary problem. Please, please think about this and then set an appointment with the social worker to talk about this. It is normal to feel lost and unsure of life after your partner of so many years dies. It isn't normal to think about taking your life."

We sat in silence. I started worrying that I had overstepped my boundaries. I knew what I said was correct, but wasn't positive that it was appropriate. After a long silence, Sally said, "Thank you for explaining that to me, Chris. I had not thought of our daughter, or how that could impact her. No, I don't want to commit suicide. I just don't want to live through the pain I know I will experience."

Jack coughed and opened his eyes. Sally quickly put her hand over her mouth, obviously concerned he had heard and understood the conversation. She rushed to his bedside and whispered something to him. He looked at her but it was a blank stare. He coughed again and closed his eyes.

Sally looked at the clock then and said, "Oh dear, it's time for me to go to the salon now. Thank you for listening to me. I do hear what you are saying. I will call the social worker tomorrow. I promise. I'll be back in a couple of hours."

"You're welcome Sally. Enjoy your time and we'll see you in a while."

I moved to the couch where I had a better view of Jack and took out my book. I read most of the time I was there. Jack didn't open his eyes the entire time. When Sally returned, she was in a much better mood. She thanked me and walked out to the car with me, saying, "Thanks again Chris. It was nice to get out of the house. I am feeling much better now. It's amazing what you and Hospice do for others. I hope you will find your reward in heaven."

"Thanks Sally. I'm rewarded by all of the people I meet and work with." She returned the smile and waved as I backed the car out of the parking space.

On the drive home I thought over the different wording to put on the progress notes. I wasn't sure how to report this visit. I decided to listen to the radio and enjoy the drive home instead of worrying about the notes. Once home, I called Mary, the volunteer coordinator, and told her about the visit. She helped me with the wording for the report. She also shared with me that Sally had called and left a message for the social worker to call her as soon as she was in the office. That was a good sign. I felt relief knowing that my conversation with Sally got through to her.

Jack died two days later without regaining consciousness. Sally left a message at the Hospice office thanking them for sending me to her home that day. She said I was a great help and wanted them to pass that along to me. Once again my heart filled with joy knowing I had made a difference.

Sun Li

Sun Li was a delightful woman in her early sixties who moved to her daughter and son-in-law's home shortly after her diagnosis of stage-four lung cancer. I was assigned to visit her once a week while her daughter completed errands and fulfilled her volunteer appointments.

My introductory visit with Sun Li and her daughter Susan felt like a visit with old friends. I felt at home from the moment I walked in the front door. Sitting in the living room we talked about Sun Li's health, and her recent move. Susan made us tea and we visited and planned that I would come on Tuesdays from 10 AM to 2 PM. After this first visit, I was excited about returning the following Tuesday.

The week went by quickly and I was happy as I parked my car and went to their front door. Susan answered my ring and welcomed me. From the entry hall I looked to the right and was surprised to see a curtain hung across the opening to the sunken living room where I had visited with Sun Li and Susan on my introductory visit. Susan said to follow her, and we walked to the family room on the other side of the house. She offered me a seat. She looked very tired and cleared her throat before she quietly said, "Chris, Mom has taken a downhill turn since you were here. She doesn't have the strength to climb the stairs to her bedroom so we moved her bed into the living room and put curtains up to give her privacy. She's sleeping right now because we had to increase her pain medication. She has been looking forward to your visit for days now and wants you to go wake her about 11. I want to warn you, she is very thin and her face is pale. She doesn't want to bother with make-up which is surprising since it has always been so important to her. I just wanted to warn you so you won't be shocked when you see her."

I remained in the family room and took out my novel while Susan went upstairs to finish getting ready to leave. She came back to the family room and reminded me that her cell phone number was on a paper on the refrigerator if I needed to call her.

At 11:00 I put my novel back into my bag and quietly went to the living room as Sun Li had requested. Before I reached the curtain, she called out, "Chris, are you here?"

"Hi Sun Li I am in the hall."

"Great! Right on time, please come in!" Sun Li said.

As I pushed the curtain back and entered Sun Li's converted bedroom, she welcomed me with open arms, asking for a hug. I was a bit surprised by that since in her culture, it is not common to hug others. I put my bag down, walked over to her bed and hugged her. "Great to see you again, Chris. Please sit down and make yourself comfortable." She pointed to the love seat.

As Sun Li suggested, I sat, noticing that she was indeed pale. However, she smiled and said, "Chris this is great. I am so happy that you are willing to sit with me while Susan goes out. She is very stressed and fearful of my passing, I can tell. She tries to hide it but I'm her Mother and I sense what she is feeling. I am not sure how to bring that up to her. I don't want her to fear my death, I don't. I am not happy that I am going to die so young, but I don't have any regrets. I have traveled extensively. I have loving family and friends. I led a very comfortable life and although my ex-husband, Bob and I had a very unpleasant divorce, we have worked through all of that and are the best of friends now. He is very upset that he is in London now, on business, and can't be here with me. We talk once a week which is lovely. We have heart-to-heart visits and we have times where we laugh and are silly together. That is how we were when we were younger and first married. It's sad to think of all the years we wasted being angry with each other. After Susan was born, Bob got more and more absorbed in his job. He worked long hours and traveled a lot. Susan and I both felt lonely and abandoned by Bob. In his mind he was being a good provider. I didn't approach the subject well, so every time I tried to talk with him to let him know how much we missed him he would get angry, yell, and leave. We just couldn't get together and talk things out."

We sat in silence a few moments and I said, "Thank you for sharing that Sun Li. I am happy to hear that you and Bob were able to clear things up and that you have a good friendship now. How did Susan respond to your renewed friendship with Bob?"

"Oh, she was thrilled" Sun Li said. "Once Bob and I were able to talk things out and have a good relationship he went to Susan and they talked for hours. They both cried and apologized for the harsh words between them. They have a close relationship now too. It's wonderful."

We continued to visit together and I made lunch for Sun Li. She was tired after she ate, so I went to the family room to read while she took a nap. She slept until Susan returned and came into the family room. "Hi, Chris. How did it go?"

"Sun Li was very happy to see me. She asked me for a hug as soon as I entered the room. We had a fantastic visit."

Susan sat quiet for a moment and then said, "That's amazing that Mom asked for a hug. She is usually very quiet and reserved and I have not known her to ask someone for a hug! You are very special."

"I was surprised and honored when she asked me. I guess she could tell that I am a hugger. I truly enjoyed my time with Sun Li today. She went to sleep about 1:00."

"Did she tell you how she is feeling about her illness?" Susan asked.

"We had a great talk and she was very open. I am not comfortable sharing what we talked about without Sun Li's permission though. I hope you understand." I said, concerned.

"Oh, that's fine. I understand completely. I felt that she wanted to talk about things with you and I'm glad that she did. Thank you so much for coming. You are great support for all of us. I am very relieved to know that you will be here with her when I go out. It is a lifesaver for me to have this four hour block of time to do things for myself, my husband, and children once a week. It helps me keep balance in my life and I don't feel resentful that I am taking care of Mom. Next week, when you come, I am going to go have a massage. I used to get them on a regular basis but since Mom got sick I stopped going. I realize now that it is very important to take better care of myself."

Collecting my bag, I rose. "Very good, Susan. I agree it is important. I like to use the instructions from the airlines, 'Put your own oxygen mask on first before assisting others'."

"Yes! I love that." Susan responded.

We walked to the front door together and she opened her arms to me, offering a hug. I hugged her and said, "Have a good week and I will see you next time." Susan nodded and closed the door gently behind me as I walked to my car.

When I returned the following week, Susan was on the front porch waiting for me. I could see that she was sad. As I climbed the few stairs to their porch she burst out crying and opened her arms for a hug. I put my bag down and hugged her saying, "What's wrong, Susan?"

"Mom has become so sick and so weak. She doesn't want to get out of bed much now. Nothing seems to interest her. She doesn't talk on the phone with Dad anymore, just asks me to tell him that she loves him. This is much harder than I imagined and it is happening much faster than even the doctor thought."

"Yes I agree. She does seem to be going downhill quickly. Is there anything I can do to help you, Susan?"

"No, just knowing that you are willing to stay with Mom has been a tremendous help. It's also nice that I can talk with you openly. Mom also appreciates feeling comfortable talking with you. You have a special way about you that evokes immediate trust."

Sun Li called out from her room, asking me to come in. Susan added, "Go on in to see Mom. I think I'll go upstairs to my office and do some work rather than going out."

I walked to Sun Li's room. Entering her room I was shocked at her appearance. She seemed so small in her bed. Although her smile was bright, her eyes told me the story. She was worn out. I approached her bed and she motioned for me to sit down. She reached out to me and I took her hand in mine, saying, "Hi Sun Li. It's good to see you."

Sun Li took a moment to respond and then she said, "Hi Chris. It's great to see you too. I have a request I hope you will be open too."

"What's that Sun Li?"

"Is Susan still here by any chance?" she asked.

"Yes. She went upstairs to do some work. Why?"

"Please get her so I can tell you both what I'd like to do today." Sun Li said.

"Ok Sun Li. I'll be right back with Susan."

She came downstairs with me to Sun Li's room. Sun Li smiled at us and said, "Susan, what I'd love to do today is have you go to the drive-thru and get each of us a children's meal that has a toy."

Susan looked at me. I smiled and nodded my head with approval. She said, "Ok Mom, I'll be right back." She left the bedroom, gathered her purse and sunglasses and left.

Sun Li started to giggle. She looked at me and said, "Chris this is so fun. I can't tell you how much I am looking forward to having a fun meal with you and Susan!"

"I'm looking forward to this too, Sun Li."

Susan returned with our meals and we set up in Sun Li's room. I was a bit uncomfortable at the thought of eating this fast food meal and then acknowledging the free toy that came with it. Sun Li opened her free toy and laughed. "Oh how fun, it's a spin top!" she exclaimed.

Susan and I also took out our tops and started spinning them. We laughed together and managed to finish our cold meals, but the focus was on being silly and playing.

Suddenly Sun Li was laughing and crying at the same time. Startled, Susan said, "Mom, what's wrong?"

Sun Li cleared her throat and said, "I'm ok honey, I am just overwhelmed with joy and a bit sad at the same time. I can't thank you and Chris enough for this very special time together."

Susan and I both thanked Sun Li and I walked over and gave her a hug. "I better go now. Take care, I'll see you next week."

With a very sad face Sun Li said, "I'm not sure I will still be here then, Sweetie." She blew me a kiss and I blew one back as I walked out the front door.

Once in the car, the sob I had been holding back, escaped. I felt the sense of loss already. No matter how long I know each patient, it is always hard to say good-bye. On the drive home I relived our day together. I was surprised at how much fun I had as we ate a simple fast food meal and played with our spin toy! I was thankful for the time together and yet felt sad.

The following afternoon Susan called Hospice and asked the volunteer coordinator to call me to share that Sun Li had slipped into a coma. They wanted me to know. By the time the volunteer coordinator finished her meetings and was about to call me, Susan called Hospice again, this time to say that Sun Li had passed.

Naturally I was sad to hear that Sun Li had died but I was grateful knowing she was now at peace. She taught me something I have never forgotten. She showed me the value of staying in the moment and being playful. In our many talks she said that she didn't ever want to grow up if that meant not being silly sometimes.

What a blessing Sun Li was in my life. I think of her often, especially when I am laughing or being silly. At these times I feel her spirit with me.

Mr. Peterson

August 18, 2004 began as any other regular day but ended up being for me, an opportunity of a lifetime. That was when I met Mr. Peterson. I was assigned to give him a neck and shoulder massage weekly. From the moment I read his intake sheet, I sensed the need to call him Mr. Peterson, rather than using his first name, which was typical with most patients. During our time together, he also never asked me to call him by any other name.

As I arrived at Mr. Peterson's front door and rang the bell, I did not remotely suspect what the next four months of my life would be like!

When he opened the door he wore a big smile and his entire face was radiant. I beamed back at him. It was love at first sight! I could see a white light surrounding him, outlining his body. It was as if I was visiting an old friend, not introducing myself to him for the first time.

As I entered his apartment I gazed around the living and dining room. Somehow it felt familiar, comfortable to me. Noticing the beautiful piano I smiled. Mr. Peterson exclaimed, "Do you like piano music?"

"Yes Mr. Peterson, I sure do. I took lessons as a young child but didn't stick with it."

We talked together for a few minutes and then moved to the other room so that I could start his massage while he sat on a kitchen chair. I began working on his neck and shoulders. His muscles were very tight and he had several big knots as well. As I worked on him, he told me how good it felt. He said that he wanted to get his muscles loose enough and out of pain so he could play the piano and organ more easily. At 87 years old, and dealing with liver cancer, he still played at his church one Sunday a month. In addition he taught private piano lessons in his home.

He sat and I stood behind him working on him. I could tell that it would be hard for me to get the knots worked out without creating soreness. I mentioned to him that it would take several treatments to get his muscles back to normal and said I did have an idea that may give additional help. I told him I was a reflexology practitioner and would be glad to give him a foot massage in addition to the neck and shoulders.

Immediately he said, "Okay!" as he enthusiastically tossed his slippers off his feet. I laughed as I watched the slippers fly across the room!

As I massaged his feet Mr. Peterson began critiquing me. I guess that is a natural thing for a teacher of more than 40 years to do. He kept telling me how good it felt and that there was something special in my hands. I could sense that he had more to say but was testing my reactions before going further with the conversation. I also took note of the fact it was impossible for him to keep quiet as I massaged his feet. This was a very self-confident man who always seemed to be in control.

After I finished his foot massage and headed to the bathroom to wash my hands he thanked me over and over for helping him so much. He continued to talk even though I left the room.

When I came out, Mr. Peterson was sitting at his piano. He gave me that beautiful smile and said, "Chris, will you stay and let me play for you? I want to offer my gratitude for all that you have done for me today."

Excitement rumbled deep within me. "Yes Mr. Peterson I would love to hear you play!"

I sat on the couch as he began. The music he played touched my soul, and the connection I found with Mr. Peterson from the minute he opened the door deepened. Tears streamed down my cheeks as the music simultaneously filled both the air and my spirit. When he finished I clapped and thanked him.

As I stood to leave his apartment he reached out and hugged me tightly as he whispered in my ear, "Honey, you are God's answer to my prayer. What a blessing you are to me."

Returning the hug I responded, "Thank you Mr. Peterson, you too, are the answer to my need." With that I gathered my bag and headed to my car.

Once in the car my tears flowed. I was filled with unconditional love. Mr. Peterson was like no other person I had ever met. On my drive home that day, I knew that visiting him was going to be a great experience.

My next visit was equally as rewarding. This time Mr. Peterson pushed a kitchen chair to the couch in front of his favorite spot. He had placed a pillow from his bed on the chair, to cushion his feet and raise them high enough for me to easily massage them. When I arrived he asked that I get another chair from the kitchen to sit on. Once we were both settled, I began his foot massage.

"Chris, I can feel energy coming through your hands and they feel warm. You have a gift from God. When you rub my feet for five minutes on each foot, I get more benefit than any of the pills the doctor gives me!"

"I am glad it helps you so much, Mr. Peterson."

Completing the massage I went to wash my hands. Returning to the living room I started to pick up my bag but he asked me to sit down. "Chris, would you be willing to visit three times a week? I think it would really help me." He requested.

Whoops! This is more than the Hospice Volunteer rules allow.

Since Mr. Peterson and I had an instant connection I was willing to come more often if I could get the volunteer coordinator to approve the extra visit. "I will have to check with the office and request permission." I replied.

Mr. Peterson frowned. After a brief silence he said, "Well why would they care how many visits you make a week?"

"They have rules and regulations we all have to follow." I explained. We visited for a few more minutes and he started to giggle. "What is so funny?" I asked.

"I am not someone who likes the rules," He said.

I knew I was in big trouble. We enjoyed our time together and he appeared to be very lonely. I told him I needed to go and that I would call him to set up our next appointment. We hugged and I headed to my car.

On my drive home, my mind raced. What was I going to do? I wanted to come as often as Mr. Peterson requested. I agreed with him that he would really benefit from the foot massage on a regular basis. At home I called Mary, the Hospice volunteer coordinator. I told her about Mr. Petersons' request. She responded immediately, "No, that is too many visits a week even if they are short visits. I'm sorry Chris."

"Okay. Talk to you later."

After writing up my progress report notes for that visit it became obvious to me that this was an unusual assignment. Although we are discouraged from getting too involved with the patient and/or the family members, this time was different. I just couldn't keep to the rules. The only thing I could think of was to go on a leave of absence. So along with my progress notes I wrote a letter stating I was taking a leave of absence immediately. I faxed the information and knew that Mary would be calling me as soon as she read the letter. Sure enough within the half hour my phone rang.

It was Mary and she wasn't pleased. "Chris I know why you are taking a leave of absence. You are going to defy me and visit Mr. Peterson three times a week. I am not sure that we can allow you to go visit him even if you are on a leave of absence. Our insurance will not cover you. This is not a good idea," she stated firmly.

"Mr. Peterson is very special to me already and I am not willing to limit my visits to him. I will continue with his foot massage three times a week."

"Chris, I have to check with management and will call you back." Mary said.

I stared at the phone receiver in my hand a moment before placing it back in the base. Sighing deeply I said aloud, "I am not going to let anyone keep me from visiting with Mr. Peterson. I will quit if necessary."

Mary called me at the end of her work day. "Chris, we have composed a letter that both you and Mr. Peterson need to sign stating that you will not be representing Hospice until further notice. Michelle (the social worker) will meet you at Mr. Peterson's apartment tomorrow at ten to get the letters signed."

"Okay, that works well for me. Thanks Mary." She hung up quickly without another word.

Mr. Peterson was very put out the next morning with the attitude Hospice was taking, but he didn't have any problem signing the letter. After Michelle left, Mr. Peterson and I talked and I gave him his foot massage. He told me that he wanted me to be the person to tell him when it was time for him to let go and die. He certainly didn't seem anywhere near death to me. "Me? Why do you want me, Mr. Peterson?" I asked.

Smiling, he responded, "Because you have the strength and training to do it. You will know when it's time. I still feel like I have a lot of work left to do here on earth. I know you will sense when it is time and I really want you to agree to help me."

I thought about what he said for a moment and responded, "Okay, Mr. Peterson, I will do that for you."

On December 13, 2004 Mr. Peterson was moved into the VA Hospital in the Hospice wing. I continued to visit him but since it was a 40 mile drive from my house, I visited only once a week. My first visit after he was moved to the hospital was on Thursday, December 16th. I brought him a lap afghan that I crocheted for him. He loved it! He had a roommate, Earl. He joked with Mr. Peterson and me. Earl suggested that I give him a foot massage, too. We had a great visit that day. I took a picture of Mr. Peterson in his hospital bed with the afghan over him. When it was time for me to go I leaned over and kissed his cheek. I told him I would call him on Saturday and come visit the following Thursday. He nodded and closed his eyes to take a nap.

On the drive home I was sad. I could see severe decline in him in five days. Although I knew that this time would come, I wasn't ready yet!

I called him on Saturday and he was sleepy and not able to hold a conversation. I told him I loved him and would be there to visit on Thursday. I called the following Tuesday and he told me that he was dreaming about Jesus. He said they were beautiful dreams. We kept the phone calls short because he didn't have the energy to talk long.

On Thursday, December 23, 2004 I arrived at Mr. Peterson's room and stopped in my tracks just inside the door. He was curled in a fetal position with his beanie cap on his head and the afghan over him. He was asleep. As I walked across the room to get a chair to put at the side of his bed, a lump formed in my throat and my eyes burned with tears. As I settled in the chair next to him I couldn't help it, I burst out crying. I gently touched his arm and he opened his eyes. His eyelids looked heavy and he struggled to keep them open. He smiled at me but didn't speak. He saw that I was crying and a concerned look came over his face.

I smiled and said, "I'm okay Mr. Peterson. This is just a 'boohoo' day for me. This is the day to fulfill my promise to you. It is okay for you to let go now. Your work here on earth is done. You can close your eyes. I'll sit here with you and we can talk if you like, but you can close your eyes."

He smiled at me, held eye-contact briefly, and nodded. Closing his eyes, he said, "Thank you honey. I knew you could do it." We sat in silence, holding hands. I cried off and on and reviewed in my mind all of the love and laughter we had shared. I was thinking that Mr. Peterson is my hero. He dedicated his life to the service of others. The only regret he had was he didn't have a family of his own. When I asked him why he never got married he said that he was so busy paying attention to other people's business that he forgot to pay attention to his own. He worked through that regret over the years but it wasn't easy. What a great example of living with purpose. Now my desire was he would die with dignity.

"Mr. Peterson today is Thursday and Saturday is Christmas. I was planning on coming to visit you about noon; will you still be here then?" I asked.

He opened his eyes, smiled and said, "No honey."

My heart sank. Tears streamed down my face. I smiled back to him, leaned forward so I was close and said, "I love you more than life. I can't thank you enough for all you have taught me. You have encouraged me to live my life to the fullest. I could never repay you, but I do thank you. I will make you proud."

Standing up then, I replaced the chair and went back to the bed. Leaning down I kissed Mr. Peterson's forehead and said, "Have a peaceful passing. Please visit me once you cross over!" With all the energy he could muster he blew me a kiss and mouthed 'I love you' to me. I walked to the door, turned and waved one more time, blowing him a kiss; I walked out sobbing all the way to the car. It was a mixture of happy and sad tears.

Christmas morning, around nine I called the VA and asked if Mr. Peterson was there. The nurse asked who was on the phone. I gave her my name and she paused, and before she could say anything I said, "He died this morning, didn't he?"

"Yes, about seven. He had a very peaceful death, Chris."

"That is great, and it's just like him to go home to Jesus, on Jesus' birthday." I responded laughing.

Later that day, Ms. Vivian, his long time friend, and caregiver called me. She wanted to be sure that I had heard that Mr. Peterson had passed away. I offered that I knew. She said that she had the afghan I had made for him and she would bring it to me at his funeral. She offered to wash it but I asked her not to. I wanted to smell his aftershave at least one more time.

Ms. Vivian went on to share that Mr. Peterson had planned his entire funeral and that I would be seated in the family section. She said he wanted me to be the second person to speak at his funeral but wanted to know if it would be okay for me to go third. "What?" I exclaimed! "I'm not speaking at his funeral."

"He said you would say that. He wants you to find a poem or two and just read them. He wants you to overcome your fear of speaking in public." Ms. Vivian explained.

I was silent for quite a while, thinking. Finally I said, "Oh that creep! Okay, I guess I better get busy looking for poems that describe our relationship. I know that is what he wants."

"Exactly! He will be so proud of you Chris." She exclaimed.

Once again Mr. Peterson was a great teacher for me. Even after his death he continues to teach me. He liked to tease and call us the "odd couple". I asked him to refer to us as the unique couple! He said we are the perfect example of what God means by unconditional love between two people. He was 87, single, and African American. I was 50, married, and Caucasian. Yet from the moment we met it was love at first sight. I lived a lifetime of joy with him, from August 18, 2004 until December 25, 2004. What more could I ask for?

I remained on the leave of absence until January 2005, when I returned to my volunteer position. I helped out in the office and had a few one-time only assignments giving foot massages to patients. In May of 2005, Dave and I moved from California to Arizona. I signed up with my local Hospice organization there and worked until May 2007, when we went to Seattle because my Mom started having so many medical problems.

Hospice remains my passion. I intend on returning to volunteering in the near future.

Section 3 –

Final Thoughts

Spread the Word

One day my friend Andrea called me with very sad news. The health issue her husband, Keith, had been fighting was finally diagnosed: bladder cancer. She said he intended to fight and beat this disease. At the age of 41 he was too young to die, and wanted to live to continue raising their children.

In talking with Andrea in the month or so after Keith's diagnoses I shared with her the benefits Hospice had to offer. We talked in-depth about the fact that Keith could have the medical attention he needed and be able to stay at home. She shared that in his culture they didn't believe in talking about death. That was a taboo subject. He wanted to do the treatment plan the doctors had suggested, which prohibits him from accessing Hospice. In addition, he felt that by signing up with Hospice he would be giving up, and therefore letting his family down. As an active and involved Dad, he didn't want his children to think he didn't love them enough to fight. He was determined to beat this disease.

Keith had surgery and went through a vigorous chemotherapy regimen. He practiced Chi Qigong daily and his health improved.

Then, much too soon, the day came when the cancer returned. I worked with him, giving him Reiki energy sessions and spiritual life coaching. We had some great conversations but he still didn't want to talk about death or Hospice. We left it that if and when he changed his mind he would tell me he wanted to talk. Then, I would give him the information to help him decide.

Although he fought a good fight, Keith began losing his battle with cancer and ended up in the hospital. Andrea was not happy with how his final days on earth went. She had regrets that he didn't sign up with Hospice, although she had complete respect for his right to make his own decision.

After a loved one passes it is common to think back on what you could have done differently to make it a less painful and more dignified passing for the patient. Often, along with grieving the loss, a survivor suffers from guilt for not doing a better job for their loved one.

Years later, Andrea called me with sad news once again. A friend of ours, Paul, had shared that he had been diagnosed with advanced stages of cancer in several major organs. He decided to fight and went in for surgery with chemotherapy planned after the surgery. During pre-op procedures the doctor discovered that the cancer had spread to the point that it was inoperable.

I asked Andrea to keep me posted on how Paul was doing, which she did. He went through radiation and chemotherapy and continued to work as much as possible.

The morning after I finished this manuscript an amazing thing happened. Andrea called me to share that Paul had passed away the night before. I knew that he had actually outlived what the doctors predicted. What I didn't know was that my dear friend had told him and his family about Hospice. She said that because she had so many regrets about how Keith's passing happened, and I had such a passion for Hospice, she kept mentioning it to Paul and his family.

She was so happy that Paul signed up with Hospice in the early stages of his fight. Once he understood that if he lived longer than the six month criteria, they would reinstate him. Because he was a patient with Hospice he was able to have things his way. His wishes were granted. He finished several projects that were very important to him and his family, which gave them all great joy.

He stayed at home and passed peacefully with his family surrounding him. I am filled with joy that he was able to die with dignity!

His family will have services available to them as they grieve, should they decide they want to use them. This is exactly why I want to get the word out about the valuable services Hospice provides!

Reflections

Living with purpose is satisfying to your soul. I have learned how to assist others without depleting myself. How to not *over* give.

The saying the airlines use; "Put your oxygen mask on first before assisting others" is a great metaphor. If I don't take proper care of myself, I have less to give to others. When I eat healthy foods, drink enough water; get enough sleep and rest I have so much more to give.

When I respond to other peoples' request with a "yes" when I really want to say "no", it is harmful to me. I have finally learned to say no when I mean it. My dear friend Marie told me that "No." is a complete sentence. I don't need to explain why I am saying it. That is great advice and advice I have struggled to take! I have done better as time goes by and when I do, it feels great. If people think badly of me for saying "no" to them, that is not my business. Another good friend, Sunny, has taught me that other peoples' opinion of me, is none of my business. What I realized about that statement is that it is just that; another persons' opinion. I have no control over what another person thinks. Therefore worrying about it doesn't accomplish anything. Just because it is that person's opinion doesn't make it true.

Living in the present moment and with integrity is what matters to me. If I'm focusing on what might happen two days or two months from now, I am missing out on what is happening right now. I've noticed that when I am in the moment I am truly available for others. I am open and able to focus.

Each Hospice assignment I took was a valuable time for me. I received confirmation that I was doing my life work; my passion. As I have written about each assignment I have relived much of it. I laughed and cried. I reflected on the lessons I learned. I felt pride in the fact that I helped many people have a peaceful and dignified death.

It is my hope that by sharing my experiences and observations that you, the reader, learned the value of the many Hospice services available. That, by reading about people who live with purpose and die with dignity, it will help you live your life to the fullest. I hope you will be encouraged to make choices for a life full of love and happiness and when the time comes, have a peaceful passing.

Time and time again, I have heard people say they don't know how I can do this work. My response; I don't know how NOT to; it is my passion. I am living my life of purpose!

CPSIA information can be obtained at www.ICGtesting.com
Printed in the USA
LVOW12s1743050913

351164LV00020B/1176/P